# House-Tree-Person Drawings:
## An Illustrated Diagnostic Handbook

L. Stanley Wenck, Ed.D.
Ball State University

*Published by*
**WESTERN PSYCHOLOGICAL SERVICES**

**WPS**® 12031 Wilshire Boulevard
Los Angeles, CA 90025-1251
*Publishers and Distributors*

Library of Congress Catalog Card Number: 76-62733
International Standard Book Number: 0-87424-147-2

Twelfth Printing . . . . . . . . . . . . . . . . . . . . . . . . . . . . . . . . . . October 2001

# Acknowledgements

The writer is indebted to Richard V. Nickell of the Fort Wayne Public Schools for his encouragement to pursue the development of the handbook and his permission to select representative drawings from the Psychological Services Bureau files. Appreciation is similarly expressed to the Anderson Community Schools Psychological Laboratory and the Regional Diagnostic and Evaluation Center of Muncie, Indiana from which drawings were also obtained.

Gratitude is owed to Kathleen Nickell, Candace Meska, Patricia Dicken, Susan Grosenbach, Rosalie Higgs and Diane Sullivan for their untiring assistance in preliminary assemblage of the handbook.

Certainly the writer is indebted to all previous researchers and writers who dealt with the use of drawings as a clinical diagnostic technique. Finally, and most significantly, gratitude is expressed to John Buck himself for the origination of the House-Tree-Person technique.

L. S. Wenck, EdD
Professor of Psychology
Ball State University
Muncie, Indiana

# Contents

# I. INTRODUCTION

**The House-Tree-Person (H-T-P) Technique and its Administration**

The H-T-P technique developed by Buck (1948) derives its nomenclature from the fact that the subject is asked to make freehand drawings of a house, tree, and person. The subject is given almost complete freedom in the manner in which he performs. Should he protest that he is not an artist, he is assured that the H-T-P is not a test of artistic ability, but that the examiner is only interested in the subject's unique portrayal.

According to Buck, the specific items—house, tree, and person—were selected because they are items familiar to children; they were found to be more universally accepted by subjects of all ages than other experimental items; and they appeared to generate richer verbal spontaneity than other items.

When projective drawings are included in a testing battery, subjects become easily involved as drawing is a favorite play behavior. Haworth and Rabin (1960) have commented that the request to draw is accompanied by a reduction of tension during the testing procedures. Subjects react to drawing with pleasure, enthusiasm, and feelings of security as it is an activity in which they feel comfortable.

The H-T-P drawing technique for which this handbook was developed continues to be one of the most frequently used projective instruments by clinicians within a variety of psychological agencies.

**Rationale and Need for the Illustrated H-T-P Handbook**

Questions are frequently asked by clinicians and students in training concerning pictorial examples of characteristics—*particularly those most difficult to visualize.* Buck's manuals have admirably served the purpose of explaining the qualitative approach to the interpretation of drawings. Examiners and students, however, must spend considerable time searching these editions for diagnostic meanings of specific characteristics. Jolles' organized catalogues (1952, 1964, and 1971) and Ogdon's handbooks (1967 and 1975) are excellent and useful aids in allowing for efficient access to interpretive data for unique drawing characteristics. Neither of the latter works include *illustrations,* however. It was felt that a need existed for an illustrated handbook which allows for rapid access to pictorial examples of a wide variety of characteristics not easily visualized and their respective interpretive significance. *House-Tree-Person Drawings: An Illustrated Diagnostic Handbook* is an attempt to provide for this need.

**General Interpretive Considerations in Using the H-T-P**

House drawings have been found to arouse associations within the subject regarding his home life and familiar relationships. Tree drawings appear to reflect projection from deeper, more unconscious levels of the personality. Wide agreement exists that human figure drawings are primarily a manifestation of the subject's perception of himself or the self he wishes to be.

Certainly, no singular characteristic should be held as conclusive indicators of the presence of certain personality traits; the configurational pattern consisting of many signs should rather be considered.

## II. Development of the Illustrated Handbook

Identification of the most diagnostically significant drawing characteristics was the first step in the handbook's construction. Perusal of pertinent literature as well as the judgment of the author and clinical colleagues were employed in making these selections. Over 180 characteristics most often mentioned in the literature and deemed most difficult to visualize were finally identified for inclusion. Characteristics easily visualized or impractical to illustrate were included in Section IX of the handbook, entitled *Non-Illustrated Characteristics with Interpretations.* Over 290 such characteristics appear in this section. Totally, over 475 diagnostic characteristics are treated in the handbook.

Permission was received to search the files of the Psychological Services Bureaus of the Fort Wayne Public Schools and Anderson Community Schools, respectively, and the Muncie Regional Diagnostic Center where the House-Tree-Person technique is employed by each staff as an integral part of all testing batteries. Drawings of children, adolescent and adult subjects referred for psychological testing were selected which most authentically represented characteristics to be illustrated. Complete anonymity of subjects' names was preserved.

Preliminary editions of the handbook were assembled in multiple copy. Feedback concerning both format and content was solicited from graduate students enrolled in projective technique courses as well as clinical colleagues. Constructive suggestions were incorporated into the current edition of the handbook. The multiple uses of this edition are outlined in the following section, *Using the Handbook.*

## III. Using the Handbook

For maximal usefulness of the handbook, users of necessity will possess a thorough background in personality theory, abnormal psychology, knowledge of defense mechanisms, and a full understanding of projective psychology. Presupposing this, the following multiple uses are available:

1. *Alphabetized Illustrations of Specific Characteristics.* Names of the characteristics illustrated are printed both at the top and to the side of each plate. Users may thumb through the handbook for illustrations of characteristics in question as one searches for a dictionary word. The Plate Index of Illustrations in section IV which follows lists all illustrated characteristics in alphabetized order with their respective plate numbers.

2. *Diagnostic Interpretation of Principal Characteristics.* Diagnostic interpretations are listed below

each principal characteristic illustrated. Interpretations listed first are presumed most valid by virtue of receiving broadest research support. Reference sources for each interpretation are indicated.

3. *Listing of Other Characteristics Illustrated within each Drawing.* In addition to the designation of the featured characteristics and respective interpretations, a list of other characteristics illustrated is carried next to each picture. Plate numbers are indicated wherein each is featured as the illustrated characteristic with their respective diagnostic interpretations. This cross-referencing aspect is intended to broaden the usefulness of the handbook.

4. *Non-Illustrated Characteristics with Interpretations.* Diagnostic interpretations of more than 290 additional diagnostically significant characteristics are alphabetically listed by category within Section IX of the handbook, entitled *Non-Illustrated Characteristics with Interpretations.* These were judged as being easily visualized or impractical to illustrate. Reference sources are listed for each interpretation cited.

## IV. Plate Index of Illustrations

## Person

# Section V.
## General Drawing Characteristics with Interpretations

### Plate 1
### Clouds

Generalized anxiety (Jacks, 1969)

Also Illustrated

(a) Lines, dark at periphery only (Plate 9)
(b) Roots, transparent as viewed from underground
(c) Sun (Plate 26)

**Clouds**      Plate 1

### Plate 2
### Details, Atypical

1. Psychosis (Mursell, 1969)
2. Unfavorable prognosis (Deabler, 1969)
3. Extreme personality disorganization (DiLeo, 1973)

Also Illustrated

(a) Lines, dark (Plate 8)
(b) Hands, omitted (Plate 149)

**Details, Atypical**      Plate 2

Plate 3  **Details, Basic Omission of**

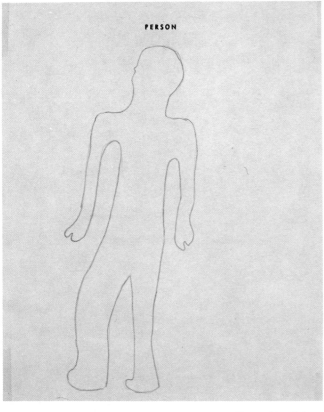

Plate 3

## Details, Basic Omission of

1. Withdrawal tendencies (Schildkrout *et al.,* 1972)
2. Hypertensive and/or psychosomatic conditions (Modell & Potter, 1949)
3. Possible organic condition (Gilbert, 1969)

Also Illustrated

(a) Hands, mitten-like (Plate 148)
(b) Shoulders, squared (Plate 172)
(c) Profile, ambivalent (Plate 170)
(d) Chin, weak (Plate 127)

Plate 4  **Details, Numerous and Painstakingly Drawn**

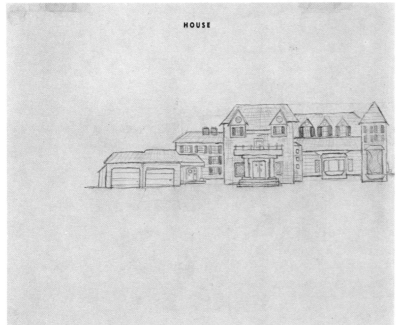

Plate 4

## Details, Numerous and Painstakingly Drawn

1. Obsessive-compulsive need to structure situation indicated; over-concern with total environment (Deabler, 1969)
2. Strong need to maintain ego control (Hammer, 1969)

Also Illustrated

(a) Shading, excessive (Plate 23)
(b) Windows, numerous panes (Plate 65)
(c) Lines, consistently straight (Plate 6)

5

# General

## Plate 5
### Groundline, Darkly Drawn

1. Feelings of anxiety and need to structure environment (Buck, 1950)
2. Extreme tension; rigidity (Urban, 1963)

Also Illustrated

(a) Branches, "wrapped in cotton" (Plate 89)
(b) Crown, cloud-like (Plate 90)

**Groundline, Darkly Drawn**     Plate 5

## Plate 6
### Lines, Consistently Straight

1. Decisiveness and assertiveness (Allen, 1958)
2. Feeling constricted by environment (Hammer, 1954)

Also Illustrated

(a) Paper-chopped drawing, bottom of page (Plate 16)
(b) Lines, dark (Plate 8)
(c) Shading, excessive (Plate 23)
(d) Animal peeping from hole in tree (Plate 69)
(e) Branches, spike-like (Plate 83)

**Lines, Consistently Straight**     Plate 6

Plate 7       **Lines, Curving**

Plate 7
**Lines, Curving**

1. Normal, flexible and healthy personality (Hammer, 1954)
2. If excessive, may indicate rebellion towards conventionality (Waehner, 1946)

Also Illustrated

(a) Lines, sketchy (Plate 11)
(b) Branches, spike-like (Plate 83)

Plate 8       **Lines, Dark**

Plate 8
**Lines, Dark**

1. Extreme tenseness (Urban, 1963)
2. Possible organic conditions (DiLeo, 1970)
3. High energy levels (Levy, 1958)

Also Illustrated

(a) Groundline, darkly drawn (Plate 5)
(b) Details, numerous and painstakingly drawn (Plate 4)

# General

## Plate 9

### Lines, Dark at Periphery Only

1. Precarious personality balance; S may be unpleasantly aware of this striving (Jolles, 1971)
2. Strong need to control existing situation (Hammer, 1969)

Also Illustrated

(a) Chimney, prominent (Plate 34)
(b) Windows, with curtains (Plate 68)
(c) Paper-based drawing (Plate 13)

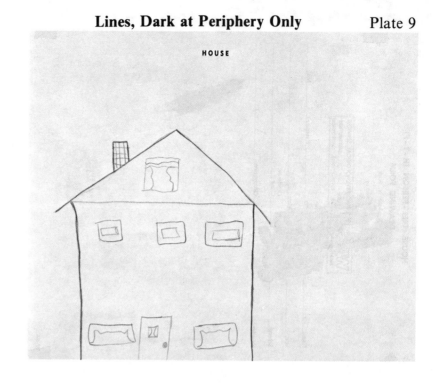

HOUSE

## Plate 10

### Lines, Jagged and Not Joined

1. Hostility (Hammer, 1965)
2. Tendency to act-out (Urban, 1963)
3. Anxiety (Machover, 1951)

Also Illustrated

(a) Arms, rigidly held to body (Plate 118)
(b) Hands, covering pelvic region (Plate 147)
(c) Trunk, long and narrow (Plate 179)

PERSON

## Plate 11        **Lines, Sketchy**

Plate 11
### Lines, Sketchy

1. Timidity (DiLeo, 1973)
2. Need for precision; meticulous (Buck, 1948)
3. Expansiveness under stress (Handler & Reyher, 1964)

Also Illustrated

(a) Branches, large in proportion to trunk (Plate 76)
(b) Leaves, numerous and in great detail (Plate 97)
(c) Paper-based drawing (Plate 13)
(d) Lines, curving (Plate 7)

## Plate 12     **Lines, Circular and Uninterrupted**

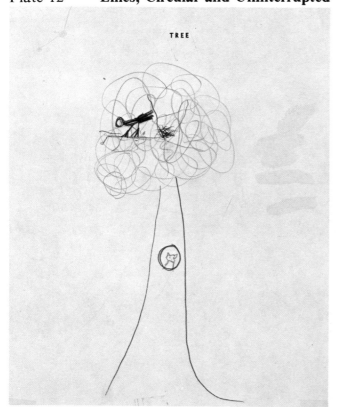

Plate 12
### Lines, Circular and Uninterrupted

Poor impulse control; confusion (Koch, 1952)

Also Illustrated

(a) Animal peeping from hole in tree (Plate 69)
(b) Crown, jumble of scribbles (Plate 93)
(c) Trunk, broadly based with diminishing breadth (Plate 107)

Plate 13

**Paper-based Drawing**

1. Feelings of insecurity; low self-
   assurance (Buck, 1950)
2. Dependency (Hammer, 1958)
3. Concrete orientation (Levy, 1950)

Also Illustrated

(a) Crown, cloud-like (Plate 90)
(b) Details, basic omission of (Plate 3)

**Paper-based Drawing**    Plate 13

Plate 14

**Paper-topped Drawing**

1. High compensatory drive levels;
   achievement oriented (Urban, 1963)
2. Excessive use of fantasy; aloof
   orientation (Hammer, 1958)

Also Illustrated

(a) Sun (Plate 26)
(b) Windows, numerous panes (Plate 65)

**Paper-topped Drawing**    Plate 14

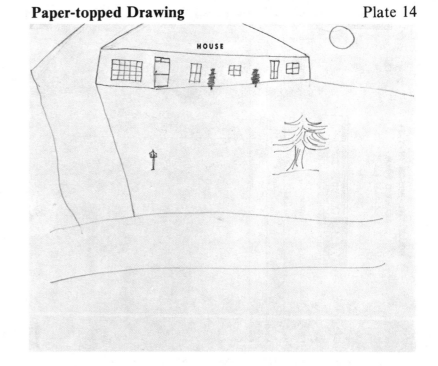

Plate 15

**Paper-sided Drawing**

Plate 15

**Paper-sided Drawing**

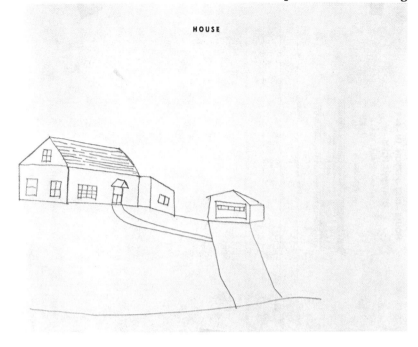

HOUSE

1. Need for a secure environment (Hammer, 1954)
2. Specific temporal meanings similar to paper-chopped drawings as in Plate 16 (Buck, 1948)

Also Illustrated

(a) Wall(s), emphasis on outline (Plate 61)
(b) Windows, numerous panes (Plate 65)

Plate 16

**Paper-chopped Drawings**

Plate 16

**Paper-chopped Drawings**

I. Left side of page

(a) Desire to cling to structures of the past (Buck, 1950)
(b) Over-concerned with oneself; self centered (Levy, 1950)

II. Right side of page

(a) Wish to escape into future to flee past (Kadis, 1950)
(b) Introversion and inner tension (Hammer, 1969)

III. Top of page

(a) S, *subject,* seeks in fantasy satisfactions denied in reality (Buck, 1948)
(b) High aspirations with low energy level (Levy, 1950)

IV. Bottom of page

(a) Need for support (Hammer, 1950)
(b) Depression of mood tone (Buck, 1948)

## Plate 17

### Perspective, Bird's Eye View

1. Rejection of symbol drawn (Buck, 1948)
2. Superiority or grandiose feelings (Landisberg, 1969)

Also Illustrated

(a) Details, numerous and painstakingly drawn (Plate 4)
(b) Shading, excessive (Plate 23)

## Plate 18

### Perspective, Worm's Eye View

1. Feeling of rejection and unhappiness (Murrell, 1969)
2. Withdrawal tendencies; Limited personal contact desired (Buck, 1948)

Also Illustrated

(a) House, small (Plate 50)
(b) Perspective, distant view (Plate 19)

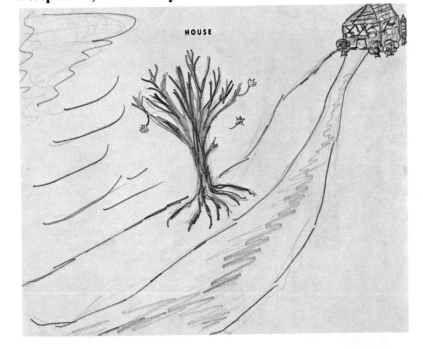

Plate 19                    **Perspective, Distant View**

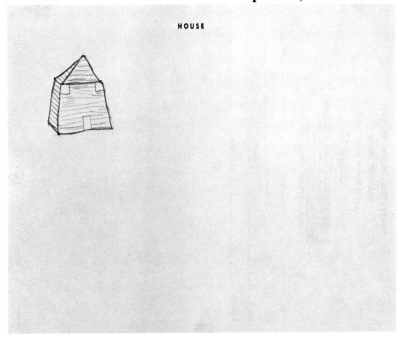

HOUSE

Plate 19
**Perspective, Distant View**

1. Regressive tendencies (Barnouw, 1969)
2. Feeling of isolation and/or rejection; withdrawal (Jolles, 1971)

Also Illustrated

(a) Lines, dark at periphery only (Plate 9)
(b) Chimney, omitted (Plate 33)
(c) House, small (Plate 50)

**Perspective, Drawing in Absolute Profile**

Plate 20

PERSON

Plate 20

**Perspective, Drawing in Absolute Profile**

1. Evasive; reluctance to communicate with others (Buck, 1969)
2. Tendency to withdraw from environment (Exner, 1962)
3. Difficulty with interpersonal relationships (Schildkrout *et al.,* 1972)

Also Illustrated

(a) Neck, long and thin (Plate 163)
(b) Hair, darkly shaded (Plate 143)
(c) Nose, emphasized (Plate 166)

**General**

## Plate 21

### Perspective, Drawing Without Profile

Tendency to be uncompromising and inflexible; possible reaction formation to felt inadequacies (Jolles, 1971)

Also Illustrated

(a) Windows, numerous and bare (Plate 64)
(b) Smoke, narrow line (Plate 56)
(c) Paper-based drawing (Plate 13)
(d) Windows, placement lacking conformity (Plate 67)

**Perspective, Drawing Without Profile**   Plate 21

HOUSE

## Plate 22

### Re-drawing of Original

1. Negativistic, aggressive reactions (Hammer, 1954)
2. Oppositional tendencies (Jacks, 1969)
3. Dissatisfaction with self (Bodwin & Bruck, 1960)

Also Illustrated

(a) Hands, omitted (Plate 149)
(b) Trunk, large (Plate 181)

**Re-drawing of Original**   Plate 22

PERSON

Plate 23 **Shading, Excessive**

Plate 23

**Shading, Excessive**

1. Anxiety and depression in elderly persons (Wolk, 1969)
2. Submissive tendencies (Allen, 1958)
3. Adjustive reaction to childhood problems (DiLeo, 1973)

Also Illustrated

(a) Space, constriction by page (Plate 25)
(b) Paper chopping (Plate 16)

Plate 24 **Shadow**

Plate 24

**Shadow**

1. Anxiety-producing conflict situation suggested (Jacks, 1969)
2. Shadow represents unsatisfying relationship of psychological past which is also currently felt (Buck, 1948)
3. If produced after sun is drawn, compulsive reactions (Hammer, 1954)

Also Illustrated

(a) Sun (Plate 26)
(b) Shading, excessive (Plate 23)

## Plate 25

### Space, Constriction by Page

1. Frustration caused by restricting environment, associated with feelings of hostility and desire to react aggressively (Haworth & Rabin, 1960)
2. Feelings of inferiority (Johnson, 1973)

Also Illustrated

(a) Paper-chopped drawings (Plate 16)
(b) Tree, keyhole shaped (Plate 101)

**Space, Constriction by Page**     Plate 25

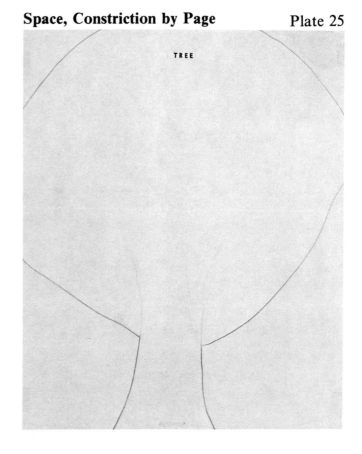

## Plate 26

### Sun

1. Inadequacy in relating to authoritative figures (Hammer, 1954)
2. Often seen as source of power and/or warmth by children and identified as father and mother (Jolles, 1971)
3. Has been produced in drawings of dependent women (Marzolf & Kirchner, 1972)

Also Illustrated

(a) Clouds (Plate 1)
(b) Door, small (Plate 45)
(c) Details, atypical (Plate 2)
(d) Perspective, drawings in absolute profile (Plate 20)
(e) Lines, dark (Plate 8)

**Sun**     Plate 26

Plate 27                    **Transparent Drawings**                    Plate 27

**Transparent Drawings**

1. Normal for young children (Machover, 1949)
2. Poor self concept in adolescents (Hiler & Nesvig, 1965)
3. In adults, poor reality contact and possible voyeuristic conditions (Wolman, 1970)

Also Illustrated

(a) House, large (Plate 45)
(b) Space constriction by page (Plate 25)
(c) Windows, with curtains (Plate 68)
(d) Wall(s), outline faintly drawn (Plate 62)

Plate 28

**Anthropomorphic Style**

1. Regressive tendencies (Meyer, *et al.,* 1955)
2. Normalcy in young children (Jolles, 1964)

Also Illustrated

(a) Details degrading to drawing (Plate 38)
(b) Baseline to wall heavily drawn (Plate 29)

**Anthropomorphic Style**      Plate 28

HOUSE

Plate 29

**Baseline to Wall Heavily Drawn**

1. Anxiety (Jolles, 1952)
2. Inability to control oppositional tendencies (Jolles, 1964)

Also Illustrated

(a) Flowers, daisy or tulip-like (Plate 49)
(b) Windows, with curtains (Plate 68)
(c) Doorknob, prominent (Plate 46)

**Baseline to Wall Heavily Drawn**      Plate 29

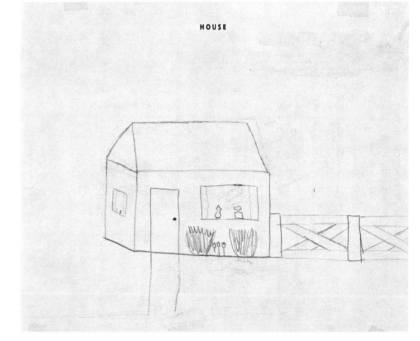

HOUSE

Plate 30                                                        **Bedroom**

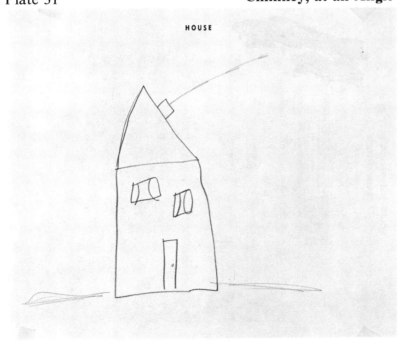

Plate 30

**Bedroom**

1. Sensitivity toward intimate and/or sexual relationships (Buck, 1948)
2. Occasionally reveals desire to escape (Jolles, 1971)

Also Illustrated

(a) Wall(s), transparent (Plate 63)
(b) Details, atypical (Plate 2)
(c) Paper-chopped drawing (Plate 16)
(d) Smoke, narrow line (Plate 56)

Plate 31                                        **Chimney, at an Angle**

Plate 31

**Chimney, at an Angle**

1. If under eight years of age, normal (Buck, 1950)
2. If over eight years of age, possible regression, mental deficiency, or organicity (Buck, 1950)
3. Probable castration fears (Hammer, 1953)

Also Illustrated

(a) Smoke, narrow line (Plate 56)
(b) Windows, placement lacking conformity (Plate 67)
(c) Perspective, drawing in absolute profile (Plate 20)
(d) Lines dark (Plate 8)

# House

Plate 32

## Chimney, Mostly Hidden

1. Partial suppression of sexual motivation (Buck, 1950)
2. Castration fears or emasculation in males (Landisberg, 1969)

Also Illustrated

(a) Door, small (Plate 45)
(b) House, small (Plate 50)

**Chimney, Mostly Hidden**  Plate 32

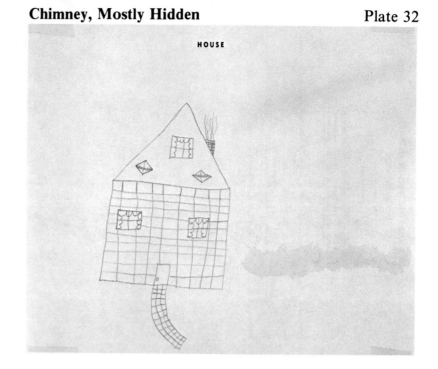

HOUSE

Plate 33

## Chimney, Omitted

1. Lack of interpersonal warmth in home (Mursell, 1969)
2. Difficulty with male sexuality, but less serious than prominence of chimney (Buck, 1950)

Also Illustrated

(a) Lines, consistently straight (Plate 6)
(b) Eaves, emphasized (Plate 47)

**Chimney, Omitted**  Plate 33

HOUSE

Plate 34          **Chimney, Prominent**

Plate 34

## Chimney, Prominent

1. Over-concern with interpersonal warmth in home (Buck, 1948)
2. Sexual concern, need to demonstrate masculinity; possible castration fears (Landisberg, 1969)

Also Illustrated

(a) Eaves, emphasized (Plate 47)
(b) Paper-based drawing (Plate 13)
(c) Smoke, narrow line (Plate 56)

Plate 35     **Chimney, Seen Through Transparent Wall or Ceiling**

Plate 35

## Chimney, Seen Through Transparent Wall or Ceiling

1. Partially suppressed exhibitionistic tendencies (Jolles, 1964)
2. Fear others may realize one's own phallic interest (Jolles, 1971)

Also Illustrated

(a) Door, above base with steps omitted (Plate 42)
(b) Shrubs, haphazardly drawn (Plate 54)
(c) Details, atypical (Plate 2)

# House

## Plate 36

### Chimney, Transparent

1. Denial of one's own sexuality, possibly due to castration and/or important fears (Jolles, 1964)
2. Female abasement of male sex symbol (Jolles, 1971)

Also Illustrated

(a) Doorknob, prominent (Plate 46)
(b) Windows, with curtains (Plate 68)
(c) Roof, single line connecting two walls (Plate 52)

**Chimney, Transparent**        Plate 36

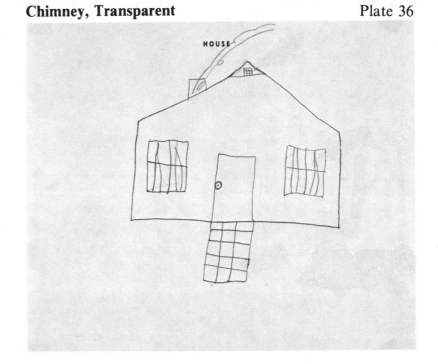

## Plate 37

### Chimney, with Hole(s)

Sex role is indistinct; fear of sexual impotency (Jolles, 1971)

Also Illustrated

(a) Lines, consistently straight (Plate 6)
(b) Chimney, prominent (Plate 34)

**Chimney, with Hole(s)**        Plate 37

Plate 38        **Detail(s), Degrading to Drawing**        Plate 38

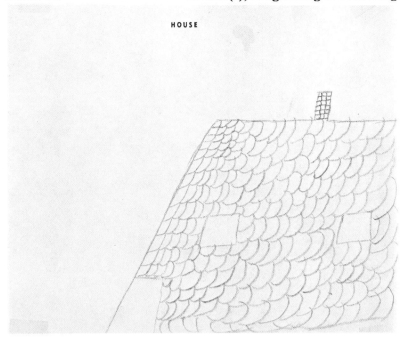

HOUSE

## Detail(s), Degrading to Drawing

1. Aggressive, hostile feelings involving family interrelationships (Hammer, 1954)
2. World seen as a dangerous place causing deliberate effort to maintain control (Hammer, 1969)

Also Illustrated

(a) Roof, single line connecting two walls (Plate 52)
(b) Paper-chopping (Plate 16)

Plate 39        **Details, Non-essential**        Plate 39

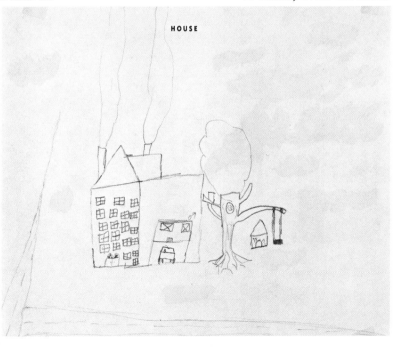

HOUSE

## Details, Non-essential

1. Obsessive need to control primary environment (Deabler, 1969)
2. Hypersensitivity regarding home and family situation (Waehner, 1946)

Also Illustrated
(a) Windows, numerous and bare (Plate 64)
(b) Door, small (Plate 45)
(c) House, small (Plate 50)

# House

## Plate 40

### Dimension, Over-emphasized Horizontal

1. Vulnerable to threatening environment (Buck, 1950)
2. Weak and fearful personality (Alschuler & Hattwick, 1947)
3. Self-protective and feminine in nature (Levy, 1958)

Also Illustrated

(a) Chimney, prominent (Plate 34)
(b) Shrubs, haphazardly drawn (Plate 54)

Dimension, Over-emphasized Horizontal

Plate 40

## Plate 41

### Dimension, Over-emphasized Vertical

1. Predominant satisfaction is found in fantasy (Buck, 1950)
2. Assertiveness and possible hyperactivity suggested (Levy, 1958)

Also Illustrated

(a) Chimney, omitted (Plate 33)
(b) Windows, omission of (Plate 66)

Dimension, Over-emphasized Vertical

Plate 41

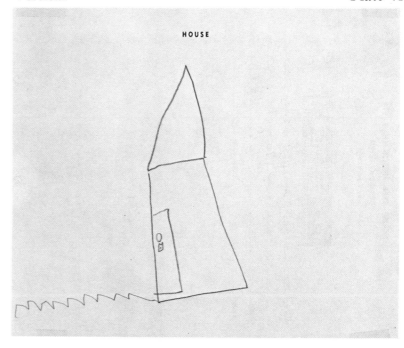

## Plate 42

### Door, Above Base with Steps Omitted

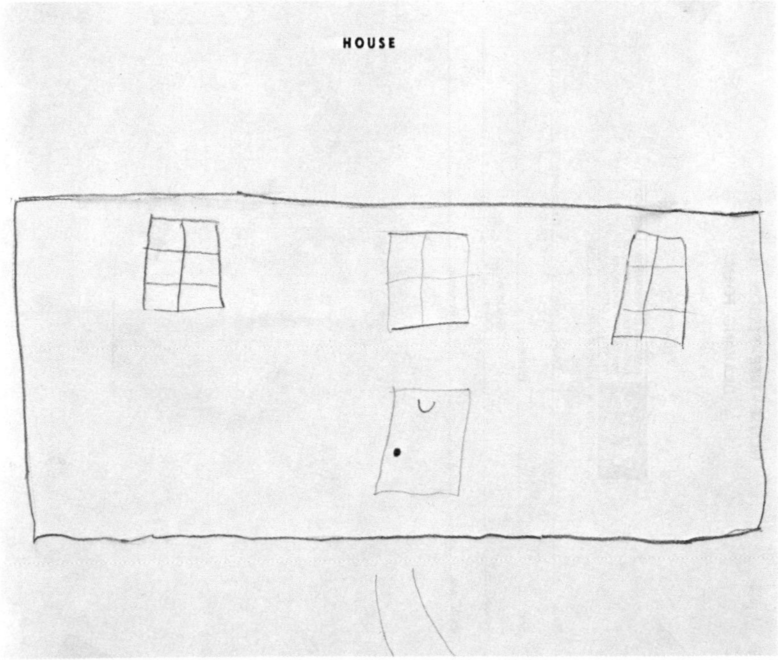

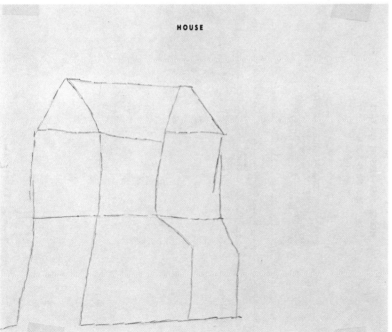

HOUSE

## Plate 42

### Door, Above Base with Steps Omitted

1. Inaccessible to others (Jolles, 1964)
2. S will contact others, but on his own terms (Jolles, 1971)

Also Illustrated

(a) Space, constriction by page (Plate 25)
(b) Roof, single line connecting two walls (Plate 52)
(c) Chimney, omitted (Plate 33)

## Plate 43

### Door, Omitted

HOUSE

## Plate 43

### Door, Omitted

1. Inaccessibility (Hammer, 1954)
2. Emotional isolation of family members (Wolk, 1969)
3. Incipient psychosis (Deabler, 1969)

Also Illustrated

(a) Windows, omission of (Plate 66)
(b) Lines, sketchy (Plate 11)
(c) Details, basic omission of (Plate 3)

# House

## Plate 44

### Door(s), Side or Back

Need to egress or escape especially when door emphasized; inaccessibility (Buck, 1948)

Also Illustrated

(a) Details, numerous and painstakingly drawn (Plate 4)
(b) Paper-chopped drawing, top of page (Plate 16)
(c) Perspective, bird's-eye view (Plate 17)

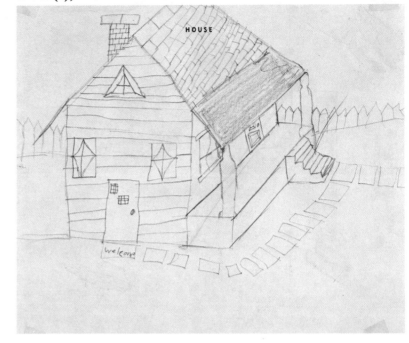

## Plate 45

### Door(s), Large and Small

I. Door, Large

(a) Tendency to rely on others (Hammer, 1958)
(b) Need to give impression of social accessibility (Jolles, 1952)

II. Door Small

(a) Reluctance in allowing access to self (Buck, 1950)
(b) Feelings of inadequacy in social situations (Mursell, 1969)
(c) Timidity (Buck, 1948)

Plate 46

**Doorknob, Prominent**

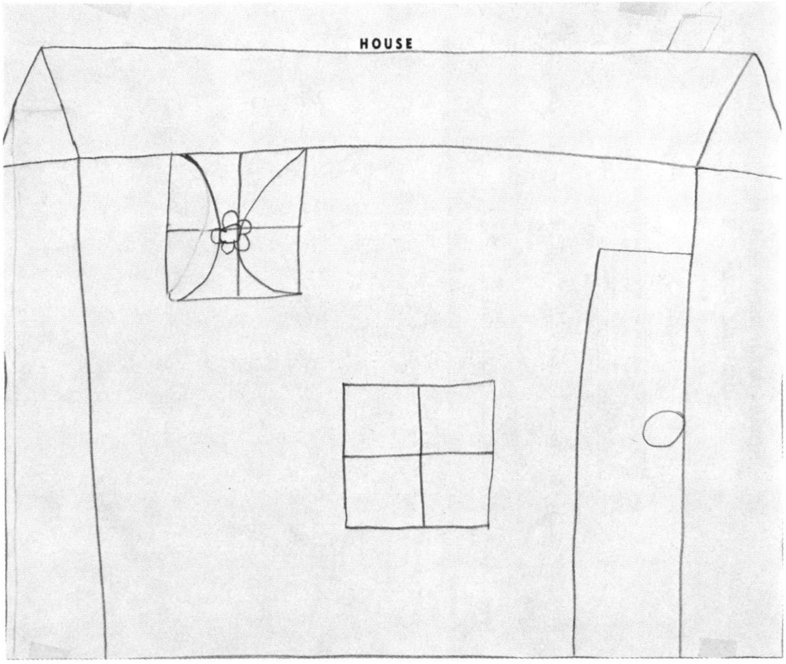

Plate 46

**Doorknob, Prominent**

Overly-concerned with social accessibility; preoccupation with phallic symbol (Buck, 1966)

Also Illustrated

(a) Space constriction by page (Plate 25)
(b) Dimension, over-emphasized vertical (Plate 41)
(c) Door, large (Plate 45)
(d) House, large (Plate 50)

Plate 47

**Eaves, Emphasized**

Plate 47

**Eaves, Emphasized**

1. Defensive attitudes and evasiveness (Buck, 1966)
2. Suspiciousness (Mursell, 1969)

Also Illustrated

(a) Chimney, at an angle (Plate 31)
(b) Windows, with curtains (Plate 68)
(c) Doorknob, prominent (Plate 46)

# House

## Plate 48

### Fence Around House

1. Need for protection from environmental threats (Jolles, 1964)
2. Need to keep inner feelings and attitudes secret (Jolles, 1971)

Also Illustrated

(a) Details, numerous and painstakingly drawn (Plate 4)
(b) Details, atypical (Plate 2)
(c) Lines, dark (Plate 8)

**Fence Around House**      Plate 48

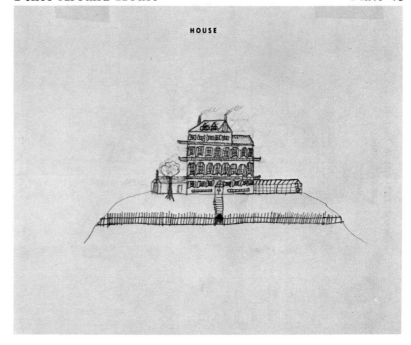

## Plate 49

### Flowers, Daisy or Tulip-like

1. Immaturity, however normal in children (Buck, 1948)
2. Regression or schizoid tendencies in adults (Hammer, 1954)

Also Illustrated

(a) Door, omitted (Plate 43)
(b) Groundline, darkly drawn (Plate 5)
(c) Perspective, drawings without profile (Plate 21)
(d) Chimney, prominent (Plate 34)

**Flowers, Daisy or Tulip-like**      Plate 49

Plate 50       **Houses, Large and Small**

**Roofs, Outlines Darkly
and Lightly Drawn**

Plate 51

Plate 50

**Houses, Large and Small**

I. House, Large

(a) Frustration, possibly due to limiting environment (Buck, 1950)

(b) Use of fantasy and/or compensatory defenses (Buck, 1950)

II. House, Small

(a) Tendency to withdraw (Hammer, 1958)

(b) Feelings of inadequacy (Buck, 1950)

Plate 51

**Roofs, Outlines Darkly
and Lightly Drawn**

I. Roof, Outline Darkly Drawn

Overconcern with controlling fantasy and intellectual activity (Jolles, 1971)

II. Roof, Outline Lightly Drawn

Fear of weakened control over fantasy and intellectual activity (Jolles, 1971)

**House**

Plate 52

### Roof, Single Line Connecting
### Two Walls

1. Mental deficiency (Buck, 1969)
2. Possible constriction of personality
   (Jolles, 1964)

Also Illustrated

(a) Details, atypical (Plate 2)
(b) Chimney, prominent (Plate 34)
(c) Windows, placement lacking
    conformity (Plate 67)

HOUSE

Plate 53

### Roof, Unusually Large

1. Fantasy satisfactions stressed
   (Hammer, 1954)
2. Introversive personality (Jacks, 1969)

Also Illustrated

(a) Door, small (Plate 45)
(b) Lines, dark (Plate 8)
(c) Windows, placement lacking
    conformity (Plate 67)

**Roof, Unusually Large**                    Plate 53

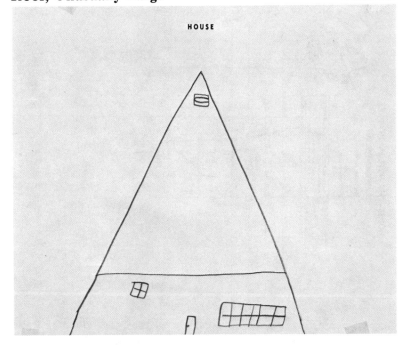

HOUSE

Plate 54           **Shrubs, Hapazardly Drawn**           Plate 54

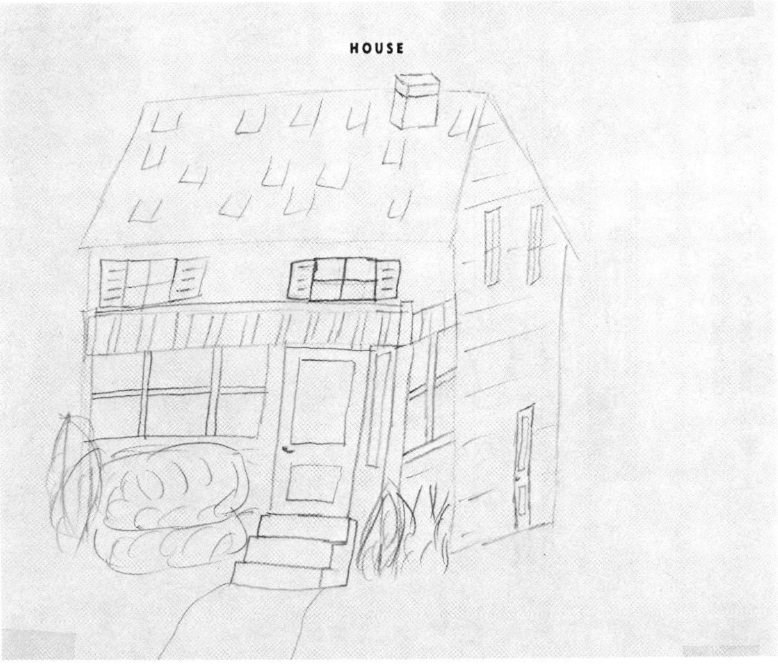

HOUSE

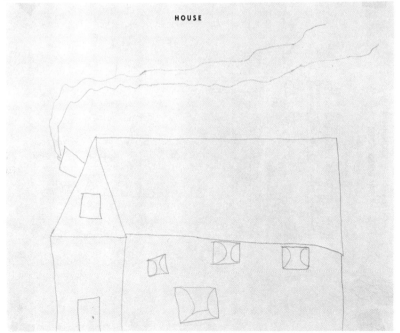

### Shrubs, Haphazardly Drawn

1. Need to erect ego defending barriers (Buck, 1948)
2. In males, defensiveness; but venturesomeness in females (Marzolf & Kirchner, 1972)

Also Illustrated

(a) Door, side (Plate 44)
(b) Details, atypical (Plate 2)

---

Plate 55           **Smoke, in Abundance**           Plate 55

HOUSE

### Smoke, in Abundance

1. Conservative attitudes if moderate left to right movement (Marzolf & Kirchner, 1972)
2. Considerable inner tension if in great profusion (Buck, 1948)

Also Illustrated

(a) Chimney, at an angle (Plate 31)
(b) Windows, with curtains (Plate 68)
(c) Paper-based drawing (Plate 13)

# House

## Plate 56

### Smoke, Narrow Line

Felt lack of emotional warmth or stimulation in home and possible urethral erotic fantasies (Jolles, 1971)

Also Illustrated

(a) Chimney, at an angle (Plate 31)
(b) Windows, placement lacking conformity (Plate 67)
(c) Windows, with curtains (Plate 68)

**Smoke, Narrow Line**     Plate 56

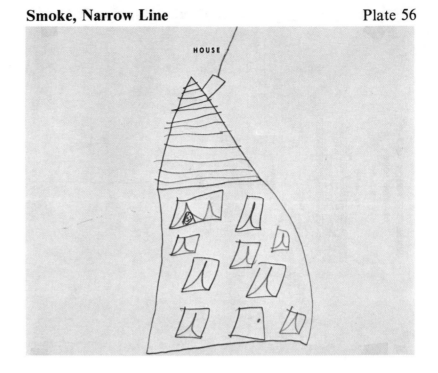

HOUSE

## Plate 57

### Steps, Ending at a Blank Wall

1. Difficulty with accessibility (Hammer, 1954)
2. Withdrawal with reality testing disability (Buck, 1948)

Also Illustrated

(a) Lines, consistently straight (Plate 6)
(b) Dimension, over-emphasized horizontal (Plate 40)

**Steps, Ending at a Blank Wall**     Plate 57

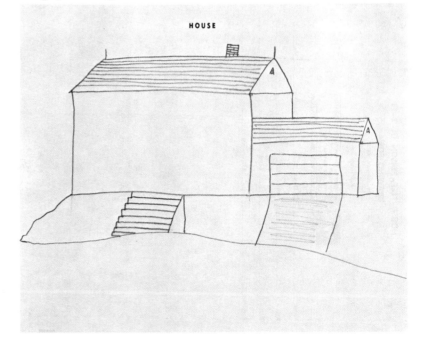

HOUSE

Plate 58             **Trees, Drawn with House**

Plate 58

### Trees, Drawn with House

1. Strong needs for reliance on others; dependency (Levine & Sapolsky, 1969)
2. Often represent specific persons of subject's family (Buck, 1948)

Also Illustrated

(a) Chimney, at an angle (Plate 31)
(b) Smoke, narrow line (Plate 56)

Plate 59        **Wall(s), Double Perspective, Thin Endwall(s)**

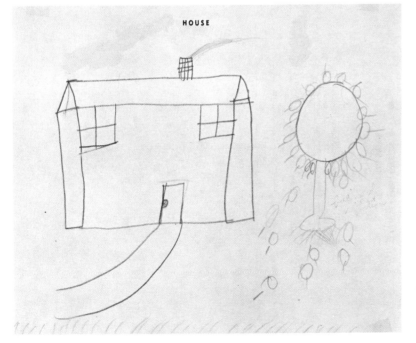

Plate 59

### Wall(s), Double Perspective, Thin Endwall(s)

1. Possible mental deficiency (Buck, 1950)
2. Possible schizophrenic regression (Buck, 1948)

Also Illustrated

(a) Tree, drawn with house (Plate 58)
(b) Doorknob, prominent (Plate 46)

# House

## Plate 60

### Wall(s), Double Perspective, Unusually Large Endwall(s)

1. Over-protective of self (Jolles, 1964)
2. Possible schizophrenia (Deabler, 1969)

Also Illustrated

(a) Lines, sketchy (Plate 11)
(b) Steps, ending at blank wall (Plate 57)
(c) Roof, unusually large (Plate 53)
(d) Chimney, omitted (Plate 33)

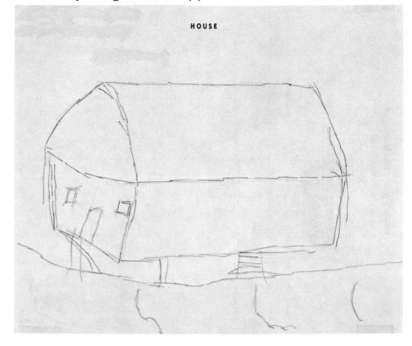

## Plate 61

### Wall(s), Emphasis on Outline

1. Conscious effort to maintain control (Jolles, 1952)
2. Need to dominate (Jolles, 1964)

Also Illustrated

(a) Windows, numerous panes (Plate 65)
(b) Wall(s), double perspective, unusually large endwall (Plate 60)

**Wall(s), Emphasis on Outline**  Plate 61

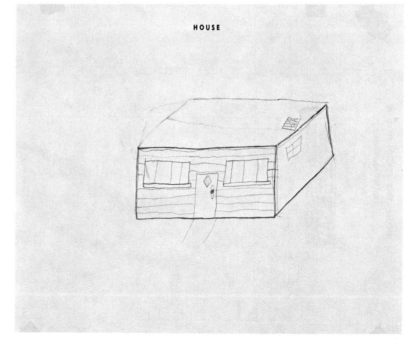

Plate 62          **Wall(s), Outline Faintly Drawn**          Plate 62

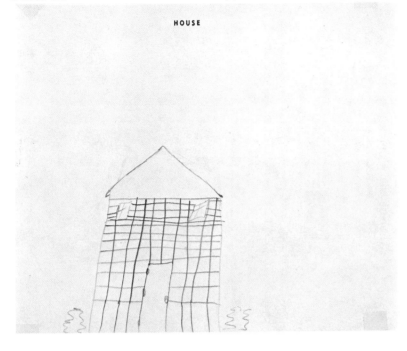

### Wall(s), Outline Faintly Drawn

Fear of impending breakdown; weakening ego control; inability to cope with tension (Hammer, 1958)

Also Illustrated

(a) Shrubs, haphazardly drawn (Plate 54)
(b) Chimney, omitted (Plate 33)
(c) Paper-based drawing (Plate 13)

Plate 63          **Walls, Transparent**          Plate 63

### Walls, Transparent

1. Impaired reality testing (Levine & Sapolsky, 1969)
2. Compulsive need to structure environment (Buck, 1948)
3. In children, normalcy indicated (Hammer, 1958)

Also Illustrated

(a) Roof, unusually large (Plate 53)
(b) Windows, omission of (Plate 66)

## Plate 64

### Windows, Numerous and Bare

1. Possible exhibitionistic tendencies suggested, especially if in bedroom (Buck, 1948)
2. Without shades or shutters, a readiness for environmental contact is indicated (Buck, 1966)

Also Illustrated

(a) Chimney, omitted (Plate 33)
(b) Door, small (Plate 45)
(c) Eaves, emphasized (Plate 47)

**Windows, Numerous and Bare**    Plate 64

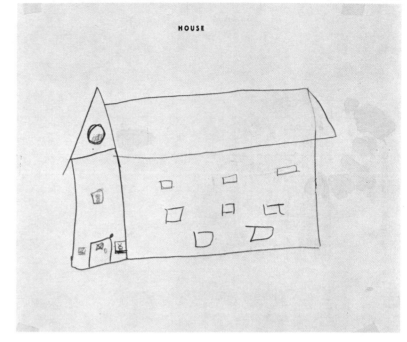

## Plate 65

### Windows, Numerous Panes

1. Overconcern for interpersonal relationships (Buck, 1950)
2. Reserved accessibility; reluctance to show feelings (Jolles, 1964)

Also Illustrated

(a) Lines, dark (Plate 8)
(b) Door, omitted (Plate 43)
(c) Details, numerous and painstakingly drawn (Plate 4)
(d) Eaves, emphasized (Plate 47)

**Windows, Numerous Panes**    Plate 65

Plate 66                    **Windows, Omission of**

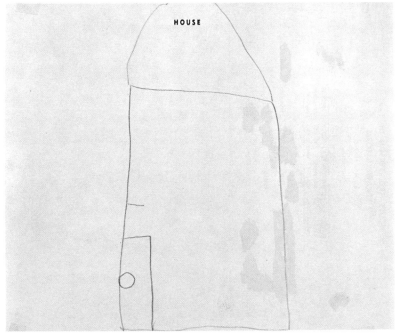

Plate 66

**Windows, Omission of**

1. Hostile tendencies (Buck, 1966)
2. Withdrawal tendencies (Hammer, 1954)

Also Illustrated

(a) Doorknob, prominent (Plate 46)
(b) Paper-chopped drawing, top of page (Plate 16)

**Windows, Placement
Lacking Conformity**

Plate 67

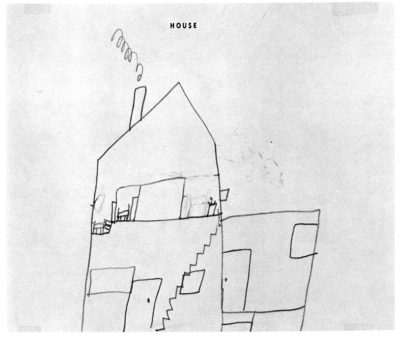

Plate 67

**Windows, Placement
Lacking Conformity**

1. Possibility of schizophrenia (Buck, 1948)
2. Possibility of organicity (Buck, 1966)

Also Illustrated

(a) Wall, transparent (Plate 63)
(b) Bedroom (Plate 30)
(c) Paper-based drawing (Plate 13)

# House

Plate 68

## Windows, with Curtains

1. Withdrawal tendencies; reserved accessibility (Hammer, 1958)
2. If not closed, consciously controlled socializing with implied anxiety (Buck, 1950)

Also Illustrated

(a) House, small (Plate 50)
(b) Eaves, emphasized (Plate 47)

HOUSE

## Plate 69

**Animal Peeping from Hole in Tree**

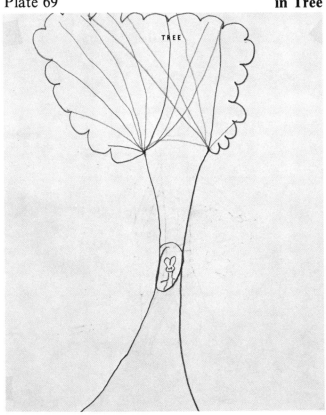

## Plate 70

**Apple Tree**

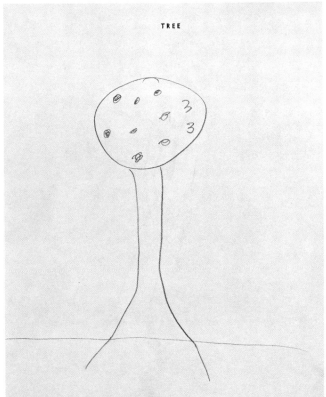

### Plate 69
## Animal Peeping from Hole in Tree

1. In children normalcy, though suggesting dependency or regressiveness in adolescents and adults (Jolles, 1964)
2. In women's drawings, may suggest outgoing, assertive personality (Marzolf & Kirchner, 1972)

Also Illustrated

(a) Crown, cloud-like (Plate 90)
(b) Lines, dark (Plate 8)
(c) Paper-based drawing (Plate 13)

### Plate 70

## Apple Tree

1. Often drawn by dependent children (Buck, 1966)
2. In persons over seven, regression or immaturity (Fukada, 1969)
3. Suspiciousness in women (Marzolf & Kirchner, 1972)

Also Illustrated

(a) Trunk, broadly based (Plate 107)
(b) Ground, transparent; roots visible below surface (Plate 95)

# Tree

## Plate 71

### Bark, Depicted as Evenly Spaced Vine-like Vertical Lines

Schizoid characteristics (Hammer, 1954)

Also Illustrated

(a) Crown, cloud-like (Plate 90)
(b) Paper-based drawing (Plate 13)
(c) Branches, shaded (Plate 81)

**Bark, Depicted as Evenly Spaced Vine-like Vertical Lines**    Plate 71

## Plate 72

### Bark, Heavily Drawn

Anxiety and hostility (Buck, 1966)

Also Illustrated

(a) Branches, "wrapped in cotton" (Plate 89)
(b) Paper-based drawing (Plate 13)

**Bark, Heavily Drawn**    Plate 72

Plate 73 **Bark, Carefully Drawn**

Plate 73

Plate 73

## Bark, Carefully Drawn

Suggests compulsiveness and over-concern with environmental interactions (Jolles, 1964)

Also Illustrated

(a) Details, numerous and painstakingly drawn (Plate 4)
(b) Branches, spike-like (Plate 83)

Plate 74 **Branches Broken and/or Bent**

Plate 74

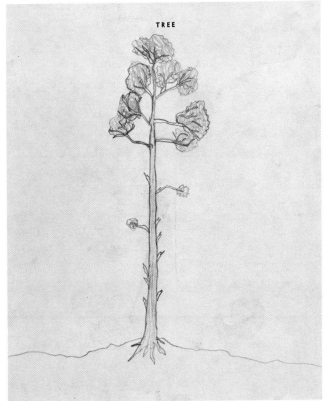

Plate 74

## Branches, Broken and/or Bent

1. Traumatic experiences suggested (Hammer, 1958)
2. Loss of satisfaction-seeking resources (Buck 1950)
3. Castration feelings (Hammer, 1953)

Also Illustrated

(a) Branches, "wrapped in cotton" (Plate 89)
(b) Roots, transparent as viewed from underground (Plate 99)
(c) Details, numerous and painstakingly drawn (Plate 4)

# Tree

## Plate 75

### Branches, in Perfect Symmetry

Ambivalence and indecisiveness (Jolles, 1971)

Also Illustrated

(a) Trunk, diminutive, with broad branch structure (Plate 109)
(b) Tree, small (Plate 104)
(c) Lines, dark (Plate 8)

## Plate 76

### Branches, Large in Proportion to Trunk

1. Compensatory, high achievement tendencies (Buck, 1948)
2. Heightened interest in seeking satisfaction from environment (Hammer, 1958)

Also Illustrated

(a) Details, numerous and painstakingly drawn (Plate 4)
(b) Branches, numerous on a small trunk (Plate 78)
(c) Lines, dark at periphery only (Plate 9)

**Branches, Large in Proportion to Trunk**    Plate 76

Plate 77

**Branches, New Growth
Extending from Barren Trunk**

Plate 77

## Branches, New Growth
## Extending from Barren Trunk

1. New hope of seeking satisfaction from environment (Jolles, 1971)
2. Possible sexual rejuvenation, especially if history of impotency exists (Jolles, 1971)

Also Illustrated

(a) Paper-topped drawing (Plate 14)
(b) Lines, sketchy (Plate 11)

Plate 78

**Branches, Numerous
on Small Trunk**

Plate 78

## Branches, Numerous
## on Small Trunk

1. Over-concern with seeking satisfaction in environment (Hammer, 1958)
2. Compensatory defenses against feelings of inadequacy (Buck, 1948)

Also Illustrated

(a) Leaves, falling (Plate 96)
(b) Sun (Plate 26)
(c) Branches, large in proportion to trunk (Plate 76)

# Tree

## Plate 79

### Branches, One-dimensional, Non-systematic and Separated from a One-dimensional Trunk

1. Inadequate and/or impotent feelings (Hammer, 1954)
2. Satisfaction-seeking resources inadequate (Buck, 1948)
3. Possible organicity (Buck, 1950)

Also Illustrated

(a) Details, basic omission of (Plate 3)
(b) Lines, dark (Plate 8)

## Plate 80

### Branches, Phallic-like

1. Overconcern with one's own sexuality (Allen, 1958)
2. Immature personality (Allen, 1958)

Also Illustrated

(a) Lines, curving (Plate 7)
(b) Paper-based drawing (Plate 13)

### Branches, Phallic-like    Plate 80

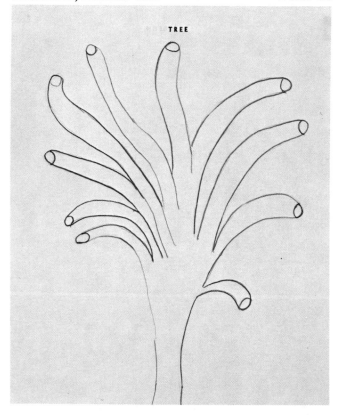

## Plate 81      **Branches, Shaded**

## Plate 82      **Branches, Small on Large Trunk**

Plate 81

### Branches, Shaded

1. Labile and insecure feelings (Koch, 1952)
2. Somatization of symptoms; agitated depressiveness (Levine & Sapolsky, 1969)

Also Illustrated

(a) Crown, cloud-like (Plate 90)
(b) Lines, sketchy (Plate 11)

Plate 82

### Branches, Small on Large Trunk

1. Frustration and inadequacy (Jacks, 1969)
2. Little satisfaction found in environment (Buck, 1969)

Also Illustrated

(a) Lines, dark (Plate 8)
(b) Branches, broken and/or bent (Plate 74)

Plate 83

## Branches, Spike-like

1. Hostile and aggressive tendencies (Buck, 1966)
2. Acting out potential (Mursell, 1969)

Also Illustrated

(a) Lines, sketchy (Plate 11)
(b) Space, constriction by page (Plate 25)

**Branches, Spike-like** Plate 83

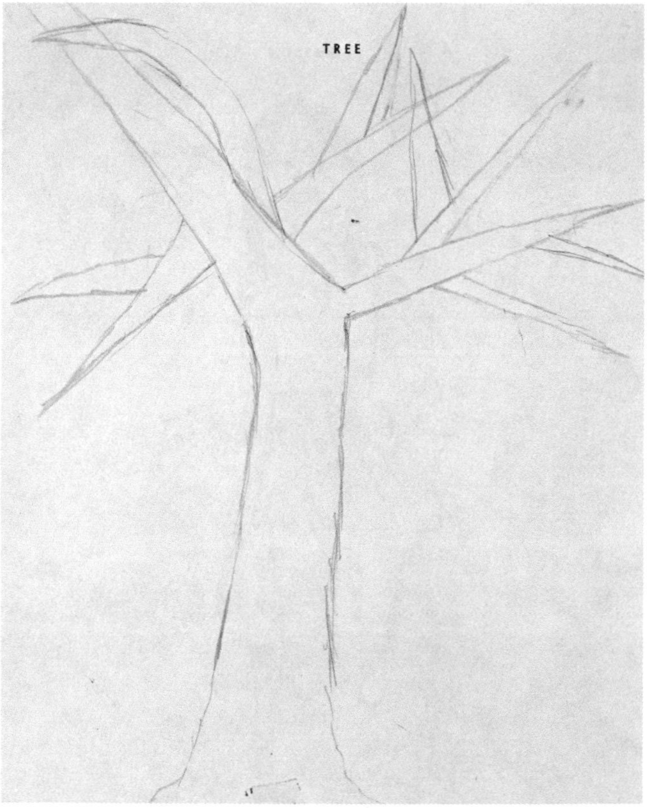

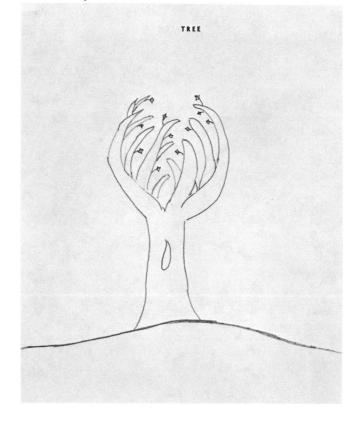

Plate 84

## Branches, Turned Inward

1. Egocentric personalities (Hammer, 1958)
2. Possible obsessive-compulsive tendencies (Buck, 1966)

Also Illustrated

(a) Groundline, darkly drawn (Plate 5)
(b) Branches, phallic-like (Plate 80)

**Branches, Turned Inward** Plate 84

## Branches, Two-dimensional with Open Distal End

Plate 85

Plate 85

### Branches, Two-dimensional with Open Distal End

Inadequate control of affect (Jacks, 1969)

Also Illustrated

(a) Paper-based drawing (Plate 13)
(b) Branches, turned inward (Plate 84)

## Branches, Two-dimensional, Club-like with Inadequate Organization

Plate 86

Plate 86

### Branches, Two-dimensional, Club-like with Inadequate Organization

1. Indicates hostility and/ or aggression (Hammer, 1969)
2. Acting-out potential (Buck, 1966)

Also Illustrated

(a) Branches, large in proportion to trunk (Plate 76)
(b) Paper-chopped drawing (Plate 16)

# Tree

## Plate 87

### Branches, Two-dimensional, Partially Drawn with Implied Foliage

1. Normality (Jolles, 1964)
2. Ability to work well with people (Jolles, 1964)

Also Illustrated

(a) Lines, dark (Plate 8)
(b) Trunk, broadly based with diminishing breadth (Plate 107)

## Plate 88

### Branches, Unshaded

Oppositional tendencies (Jolles, 1971)

Also Illustrated

(a) Roots, transparent as viewed from underground (Plate 99)
(b) Paper-chopped drawing (Plate 16)
(c) Crown, cloud-like (Plate 90)

### Branches, Unshaded — Plate 88

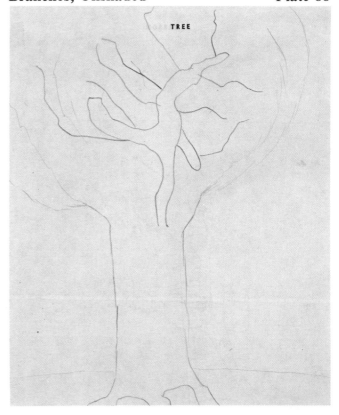

## Plate 89      Branches, "Wrapped in Cotton"

Plate 89

### Branches, "Wrapped in Cotton"

Guilt and inhibition regarding discharge of aggression (Jolles, 1971)

Also Illustrated

(a) Shading, excessive (Plate 23)
(b) Branches, two dimensional, partially drawn with implied foliage (Plate 87)

## Plate 90      Crown, Cloud-like

Plate 90

### Crown, Cloud-like

1. Use of fantasy with avoidance of reality (Koch, 1952)
2. Low energy level (Koch, 1952)

Also Illustrated

(a) Branches, unshaded (Plate 88)
(b) Clouds (Plate 1)

Plate 91

## Crown, Curlicue

1. Talkative and actively social (Koch, 1952)
2. When lines emphasized, tension and/or confusion indicated (Landisberg, 1969)

Also Illustrated

(a) Lines, dark on periphery only (Plate 9)
(b) Apple tree (Plate 70)

**Crown, Curlicue** Plate 91

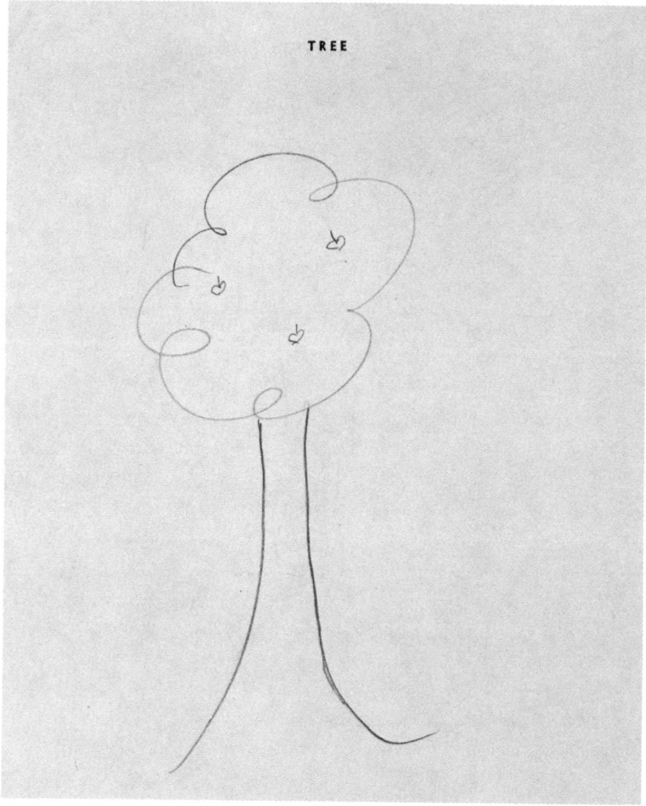

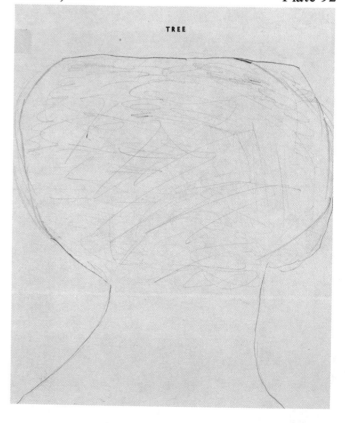

Plate 92

## Crown, Flat

1. Pressures and inhibitions in environment (Koch, 1952)
2. Feelings of hopelessness (Koch, 1952)

Also Illustrated

(a) Space, constriction by page (Plate 25)
(b) Crown, shaded (Plate 94)

**Crown, Flat** Plate 92

**Crown, Jumble of Scribbled Lines**

Plate 93

Plate 93

TREE

## Crown, Jumble of Scribbled Lines

1. Confusion and excitement (Koch, 1952)
2. Impulsive and labile temperament (Koch, 1952)

Also Illustrated

(a) Trunk broadly based with diminishing breadth (Plate 107)
(b) Branches, large in proportion to trunk (Plate 76)

Plate 94

Crown, Shaded

TREE

Plate 94

## Crown, Shaded

In maladjustive profile, suggests nervousness, insecurity, and depressive tendencies (Koch, 1952)

Also Illustrated

(a) Apple tree (Plate 70)
(b) Groundline, darkly drawn (Plate 5)

# Tree

## Plate 95

### Ground, Transparent: Roots Visible Below Surface

1. Impairment of reality orientation (Buck, 1966)
2. Schizoid thinking (Hammer, 1958)

Also Illustrated

(a) Groundline, darkly drawn (Plate 5)
(b) Sun (Plate 26)
(c) Paper-chopped drawing (Plate 16)

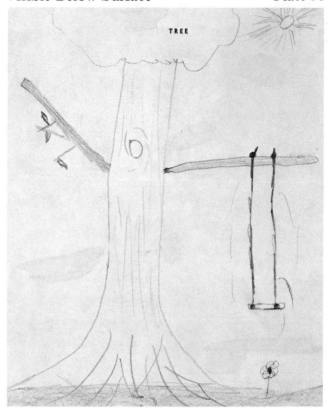

## Plate 96

### Leaves, Falling

1. Loss of ability to conform to society's demands (Jolles, 1964)
2. Loss of capacity to mask thoughts and feelings and adjust to environs (Jolles, 1971)

Also Illustrated

(a) Lines, sketchy (Plate 11)
(b) Sun (Plate 26)

Plate 97

**Leaves, Numerous and
in Great Detail**

Plate 97

**Leaves, Numerous and
in Great Detail**

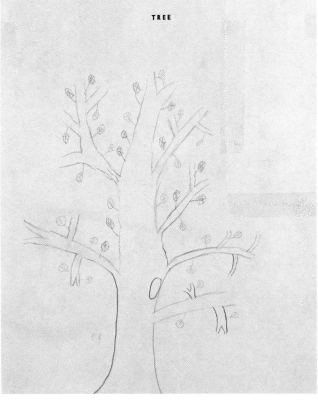

TREE

Meticulous and compulsive need to be
productive and fruitful (Levine &
Sapolsky, 1969)

Also Illustrated

(a) Branches, two dimensional, with open
distal end (Plate 85)
(b) Lines, sketchy (Plate 11)
(c) Paper-based drawing (Plate 16)

Plate 98

**Roots, Talon-shaped,
Not Penetrating Earth**

Plate 98

**Roots, Talon-shaped,
Not Penetrating Earth**

TREE

1. Impaired reality contact (Hammer,
1954)
2. Suggests paranoid aggressiveness
(Jolles, 1971)

Also Illustrated

(a) Sun (Plate 26)
(b) Branches, unshaded (Plate 88)
(c) Crown, cloud-like (Plate 90)

# Tree

## Plate 99

### Roots, Transparent as Viewed From Underground

1. Impairment of reality orientation (Buck, 1966)
2. Schizoid thinking (Hammer, 1958)

Also Illustrated

(a) Branches, large in proportion to trunk (Plate 76)
(b) Branches, numerous on small trunk (Plate 78)

### Roots, Transparent as Viewed from Underground          Plate 99

## Plate 100

### Sun, Setting Beneath Tree

Depressiveness and loss of environmental support (Jolles, 1971)

Also Illustrated

(a) Details, numerous and painstakingly drawn (Plate 4)
(b) Branches, two-dimensional, partially drawn with implied foliage (Plate 87)

### Sun, Setting Beneath Tree          Plate 100

Plate 101 **Tree, Keyhole-shaped**

Plate 102 **Tree, Nigg's**

Plate 101

**Tree, Keyhole-shaped**

1. Oppositional and possible internalized negativistic attitudes (Jacks, 1969)
2. Minimal motivation to perform to potential (Hammer, 1958)

Also Illustrated

(a) Paper-based drawing (Plate 13)
(b) Crown, cloud-like (Plate 90)

Plate 102

**Tree, Nigg's**

Indicates hostile encapsulated personality (Mursell, 1969)

Also Illustrated

(a) Lines, dark (Plate 8)
(b) Groundline, darkly drawn (Plate 5)

# Tree

## Plate 103

### Tree, Phallic-style

Sexual immaturity and/or phallic preoccupation by males over nine or ten years (Allen, 1958)

Also Illustrated

(a) Lines, dark (Plate 8)
(b) Crown, cloud-like (Plate 90)

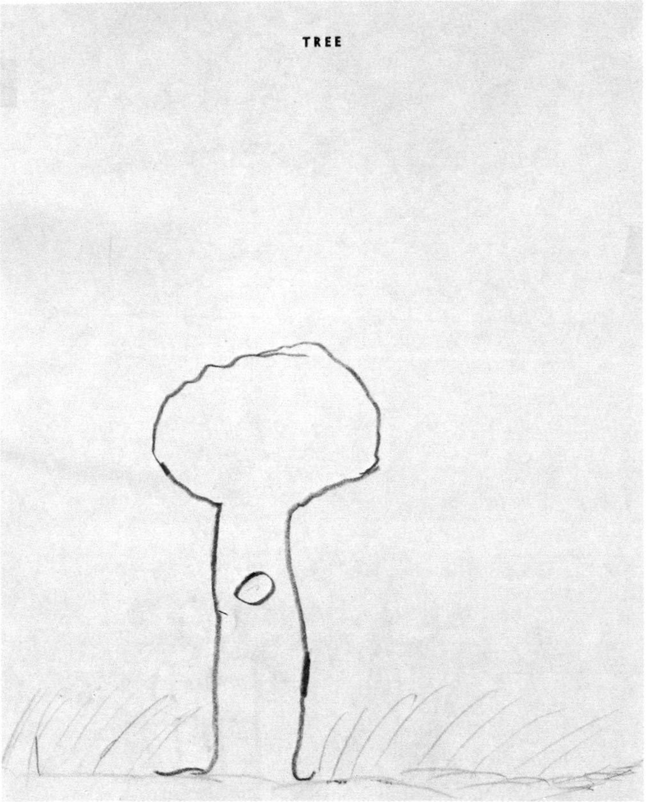

## Plate 104

### Tree, Small

1. Low energy level; weak ego (Hammer, 1958)
2. Feelings of inadequacy and inferiority (Hammer, 1954)
3. Withdrawal tendencies (Buck, 1969)

Also Illustrated

(a) Lines, sketchy (Plate 11)
(b) Lines, dark at periphery only (Plate 9)

TREE

TREE

## Plate 105

### Trees, Two One-dimensional, Drawn as One

### Plate 105

### Trees, Two One-dimensional, Drawn as One

1. Affect and intellectual pathology dichotomized (Jolles, 1971)
2. Indicates organicity (Jolles, 1971)

Also Illustrated

(a) Details, basic omission of (Plate 3)
(b) Lines, curving (Plate 7)

## Plate 106

### Trunk, Broad with Diminutive Branch Structure

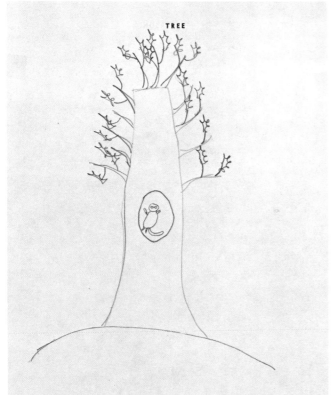

### Plate 106

### Trunk, Broad with Diminutive Branch Structure

1. Debilitating frustration regarding satisfaction of basic needs (Buck, 1966)
2. Feelings of environmental constriction and aggressive tendencies (Buck, 1950)

Also Illustrated

(a) Details atypical (Plate 2)
(b) Animal peeping from hole in tree (Plate 69)

# Tree

## Plate 107

### Trunk, Broadly Based with Diminishing Breadth

1. Oral dependent needs (Levine & Sapolsky, 1969)
2. Inhibition and/or faulty comprehension suggested (Koch, 1952)

Also Illustrated

(a) Lines, dark (Plate 8)
(b) Crown, cloud-like (Plate 90)

**Trunk, Broadly Based with Diminishing Breadth**  Plate 107

**Trunk, One-dimensional, with Disorganized One-dimensional Branches**  Plate 108

## Plate 108

### Trunk, One-dimensional with Disorganized One-dimensional Branches

1. Indications of organicity (Buck, 1950)
2. Feelings of sexual impotency, hopelessness, low ego strength (Jolles, 1964)

Also Illustrated

(a) Lines, dark (Plate 8)
(b) Lines, curving (Plate 7)
(c) Branches, numerous on small trunk (Plate 78)

**Plate 109**

**Trunk, Diminutive, with
Broad Branch Structure**

TREE

Plate 109

**Trunk, Diminutive, with
Broad Branch Structure**

1. Sees confidence and eagerness; possible over-ambition (Koch, 1952)
2. Pride with possible conceit (Koch, 1952)

Also Illustrated

(a) Ground transparent; roots visible below surface (Plate 95)
(b) Crown, cloud-like (Plate 90)

.10

, **Akimbo**

Narcissistic orientation; tendency to be "bossy" (Machover, 1949)

Also Illustrated

(a) Profile, ambivalent (Plate 170)
(b) Belt, darkly shaded (Plate 122)
(c) Chin, prominent (Plate 126)

**Arms, Akimbo**　　　　　Plate 110

## Plate 111

### Arms, Across Chest

1. Suspiciousness; hostile attitude (Urban, 1963)
2. Passive, non-assertive orientation (DiLeo, 1973)
3. In female drawing, denial of secondary sex characteristics and feeling of rejection (Machover, 1949)

Also Illustrated

(a) Feet, unusually small (Plate 137)
(b) Mouth, large (Plate 161)

**Arms, Across Chest**　　　　　Plate 111

Plate 112       **Arms, Behind Back**

Plate 113       **Arms, Held Limp at Sides**

Plate 112

## Arms, Behind Back

1. Reluctance regarding openness (Urban, 1963)
2. Need for greater control of aggressive and hostile drives (Urban, 1963)

Also Illustrated

(a) Belt, darkly shaded (Plate 122)
(b) Stance, broad (Plate 175)
(c) Shoulders, unusually large (Plate 173)

Plate 113

## Arms, Held Limp at Sides

Ineffective personality (Levy, 1950)

Also Illustrated

(a) Eyes, hollow and empty (Plate 130)
(b) Buttons, emphasized (Plate 125)
(c) Fingers, short and rounded (Plate 142)

**Person**

## Plate 114

### Arms, Large

1. Active, aggressive role in environment (Koppitz, 1966)
2. Need for strength and power (Brown, 1953)

Also Illustrated

(a) Hair, long and unshaded (Plate 144)
(b) Fingers, short and rounded (Plate 142)
(c) Eyes, unusually large or reinforced (Plate 132)

PERSON

## Plate 115

### Arms, Muscular

1. Power strivings, usually of a physical nature associated with aggression (Shneidman, 1958)
2. Acquisitive and compensatory ambition; need for physical strength, and aggressive contact with environment (Machover, 1958)

Also Illustrated

(a) Arms, large (Plate 114)
(b) Eyes, hollow and empty (Plate 130)
(c) Eyes, small (Plate 133)

PERSON

Plate 116      **Arms, Unusually Long**

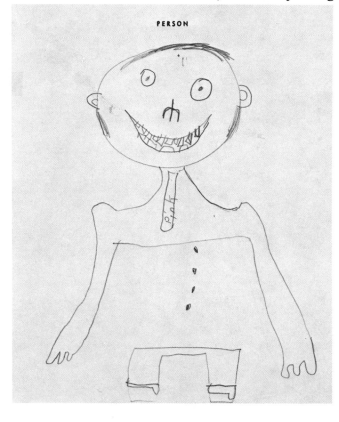

PERSON

Plate 116

**Arms, Unusually Long**

1. Achievement striving (Urban, 1963)
2. Protective mother needed (Levy, 1958)

Also Illustrated

(a) Trunk, omitted (Plate 180)
(b) Nose emphasized (Plate 166)
(c) Teeth, prominently displayed (Plate 178)
(d) Eyes, unusually large or reinforced (Plate 132)

Plate 117      **Arms, Relaxed**

PERSON

Plate 117

**Arms, Relaxed**

Dealing positively with interpersonal relationships (Jolles, 1971)

Also Illustrated

(a) Profile, complete (Plate 169)
(b) Hair, darkly shaded (Plate 143)

**Person**

## Plate 118

### Arms, Rigidly Held to Body

1. Rigid personality (Buck, 1950)
2. Compulsive, inhibited personality suggested (Schildkrout *et al.,* 1972)

Also Illustrated

(a) Lines, sketchy (Plate 11)
(b) Belt, darkly shaded (Plate 122)

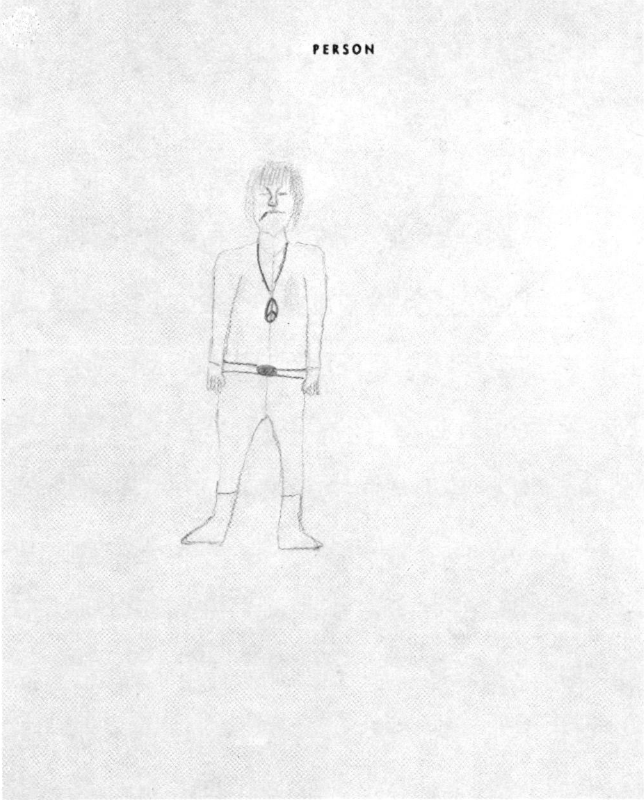

## Plate 119

### Arms, Short

1. Lack of striving or ambition with feelings of inadequacy (Wolk, 1969)
2. Passive dependency suggested (Gilbert, 1969)

Also Illustrated

(a) Hands, omitted (Plate 149)
(b) Head, unusually large (Plate 155)

PERSON

PERSON

Plate 120                    **Arms, Thin and Frail**

Plate 121                    **Arms, Wing-like**

Plate 120

**Arms, Thin and Frail**

1. Feelings of weakness (Brown, 1953)
2. Feelings of inadequacy (Reznikoff & Tomblen, 1956)
3. Possible organicity (Mursell, 1969)

Also Illustrated

(a) Lines, sketchy (Plate 11)
(b) Belt, darkly shaded (Plate 122)

Plate 121

**Arms, Wing-like**

1. Schizoid processes (Hammer, 1954)
2. Feathers present suggest schizophrenia (Buck, 1966)

Also Illustrated

(a) Details, numerous and painstakingly drawn (Plate 4)
(b) Eyes, pupils omitted (Plate 131)

# Person

## Plate 122

### Belt, Darkly Shaded

1. Sexual preoccupation suggested (Gilbert, 1969)
2. Conflict over control and expression of sexual and/or other body drives (Urban, 1963)

Also Illustrated

(a) Buttons, emphasized (Plate 125)
(b) Feet, unusually long (Plate 136)

## Plate 123

### Breasts, Emphasized

1. Psychosexual and emotional immaturity in males (Levy, 1958)
2. Probable strong oral and maternal dependency needs in males (Urban, 1963)
3. Identification with a dominant and productive mother image in females (Machover, 1951)
4. Possible exhibitionism or narcissism in females (McElhaney, 1969)

Also Illustrated

(a) Lines, sketchy (Plate 11)
(b) Eyes, unusually large or reinforced (Plate 132)

Plate 124       **Buttocks, Emphasized**

PERSON

Plate 124

## Buttocks, Emphasized

1. Immaturity and/or sexual fixation (Urban, 1963)
2. Homosexual tendencies (DiLeo, 1973)
3. If shaded, anxiety regarding homosexual tendencies (Hammer, 1958)

Also Illustrated

(a) Lines, sketchy (Plate 11)
(b) Profile, ambivalent (Plate 170)

Plate 125       **Buttons, Emphasized or Numerous**

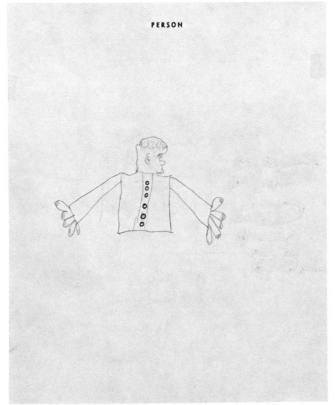

PERSON

Plate 125

## Buttons, Emphasized or Numerous

1. Immaturity (Schildkrout *et al.,* 1972)
2. When drawn compulsively, regression (Wolk, 1969)
3. When midline is emphasized, preoccupation with self and/or somatic disorders is suspected (Urban, 1963)

Also Illustrated

(a) Profile, ambivalent (Plate 170)
(b) Arms, overly long (Plate 116)
(c) Head, with irregular contour (Plate 153)

# Person

## Plate 126

### Chin, Prominent

1. Aggressive, dominant tendencies (McElhaney, 1969)
2. Strong drive level (Levy, 1958)
3. Compensatory strivings for feelings of weakness, (Machover, 1949)

Also Illustrated

(a) Shoulders, squared (Plate 172)
(b) Neck, short and thick (Plate 165)

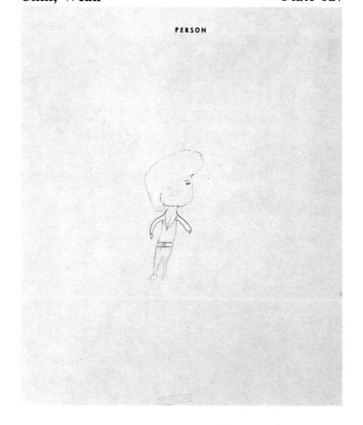

## Plate 127

### Chin, Weak

1. Feelings of inadequacy in social situations (Urban, 1963)
2. Feelings of psychological or physical impotence (Buck, 1966)

Also Illustrated

(a) Hair, long and unshaded (Plate 144)
(b) Legs, unusually short (Plate 160)

**Chin, Weak**　　　　Plate 127

Plate 128                **Chinline, Omitted**

Plate 128
### Chinline, Omitted

Basic body drives inadequately controlled (Jolles, 1971)

Also Illustrated

(a) Person running in controlled situation (Plate 168)
(b) Perspective, drawing in absolute profile (Plate 20)

Plate 129                **Ears, Emphasized**

Plate 129

### Ears, Emphasized

1. Possible auditory handicap with associated concern (Levy, 1958)
2. Accented sensitivity to criticism (Machover, 1951)
3. Ideas of reference (Landisberg, 1969)
4. Auditory hallucinations (Deabler, 1969)

Also Illustrated

(a) Lines, dark (Plate 8)
(b) Buttons, emphasized or numerous (Plate 125)

# Person

## Plate 130

### Eyes, Hollow and Empty

1. Introversive self-absorbing tendancy, (Levine & Sapolsky, 1969)
2. Withdrawn individuals who vaguely perceive external environment (Kahn & Giffen, 1960)
3. May be normal in young children (Koppitz, 1968)

Also Illustrated

(a) Eyes, pupils omitted (Plate 131)
(b) Mouth, unusually large (Plate 161)

## Plate 131

### Eyes, Pupils Omitted

Guilt regarding voyeuristic tendencies (Jolles, 1971)

Also Illustrated

(a) Belt, darkly shaded (Plate 122)
(b) Neck, omitted (Plate 164)
(c) Hair, darkly shaded (Plate 143)

Plate 132

## Eyes, Unusually Large or Reinforced

PERSON

Plate 132

## Eyes, Unusually Large or Reinforced

1. Suspicion, perhaps paranoid tendencies (Schildkrout *et al.*, 1972)
2. Anxiety (Machover, 1958)
3. Overly sensitive to social opinion (Machover, 1958)

Also Illustrated

(a) Head, unusually large (Plate 155)
(b) Neck, long and thin (Plate 163)
(c) Hands, omitted (Plate 149)

Plate 133

## Eyes, Unusually Small

PERSON

Plate 133

## Eyes, Unusually Small

1. Introversion (Machover, 1949)
2. Self absorption, introspective tendencies (Urban, 1963)
3. Reaction formation against voyeuristic tendencies (Schildkrout *et al.*, 1972)

Also Illustrated

(a) Mouth, unusually large (Plate 161)
(b) Neck, omitted (Plate 164)

**Person**

## Plate 134

### Facial Features, Omitted
### When Rest Adequately Drawn

1. Interpersonal relationships superficial (Urban, 1963)
2. Contact with environment lacking; tendency to withdraw (McElhaney, 1969)
3. Overly cautious; timid (Machover, 1949)

Also Illustrated

(a) Legs, short (Plate 160)
(b) Neck, long and thin (Plate 163)

PERSON

## Plate 135

### Facial Features,
### Overemphasized

1. Overly sensitive about appearance (Jolles, 1964)
2. Compensatory defenses of aggression and social dominance due to felt inadequacies (Machover, 1949)

Also Illustrated

(a) Shoulders, unusually large (Plate 173)
(b) Buttons, emphasized or numerous (Plate 125)
(c) Stance, broad (Plate 175)

PERSON

Plate 136       **Feet, Unusually Long**

Plate 136

**Feet, Unusually Long**

1. Strong security needs (Buck, 1950)
2. Need to demonstrate virility; castration fears (Urban, 1963)

Also Illustrated

(a) Stance, broad (Plate 175)
(b) Trunk, long and narrow (Plate 179)

Plate 137       **Feet, Unusually Small**

Plate 137

**Feet, Unusually Small**

1. Constriction; dependence (Brown, 1958)
2. Various psychosomatic conditions (DiLeo, 1973)

Also Illustrated

(a) Eyes unusually large or reinforced (Plate 132)
(b) Head, unusually large (Plate 155)

**Person**

## Plate 138

### Fingers, Long and Spike-like

1. Primitive aggressive tendencies (Goldstein & Rawn, 1957)
2. Associated with paranoid processes, psychosomatic disorders, and hypertensiveness (Shneidman, 1958)

Also Illustrated

(a) Lines, dark (Plate 8)
(b) Neck, long and thin (Plate 163)

**Fingers, Long and Spike-like**    Plate 138

## Plate 139

### Fingers, One-dimensional, Enclosed by Circle

Aggressive impulses consciously suppressed (Jolles, 1971)

Also Illustrated

(a) Details, numerous and painstakingly drawn (Plate 4)
(b) Nose, emphasized (Plate 166)
(c) Fingers, long and spike-like (Plate 138)

**Fingers, One-dimensional, Enclosed by Circle**    Plate 139

Plate 140

**Fingers, Reinforced or
Darkly Shaded**

PERSON

Plate 140

**Fingers, Reinforced or
Darkly Shaded**

Guilt possibly associated with
masturbation or stealing (Urban, 1963)

Also Illustrated

(a) Fingers, long and spike-like (Plate 138)
(b) Neck, omitted (Plate 164)

Plate 141

**Fingers, Scribbled**

PERSON

Plate 141

**Fingers, Scribbled**

Possible organicity (Reznikoff and
Tomblen, 1956)

Also Illustrated

(a) Belt, darkly shaded (Plate 122)
(b) Fingers, reinforced or darkly shaded
(Plate 140)

Plate 142

## Fingers, Short and Rounded

1. Emotional immaturity (Gurvitz, 1951)
2. Feelings of inadequacy (Schildkrout *et al.,* 1972)

Also Illustrated

(a) Neck, long and thin (Plate 163)
(b) Feet, unusually small (Plate 137)
(c) Head, unusually large (Plate 155)

**Fingers, Short and Rounded** Plate 142

PERSON

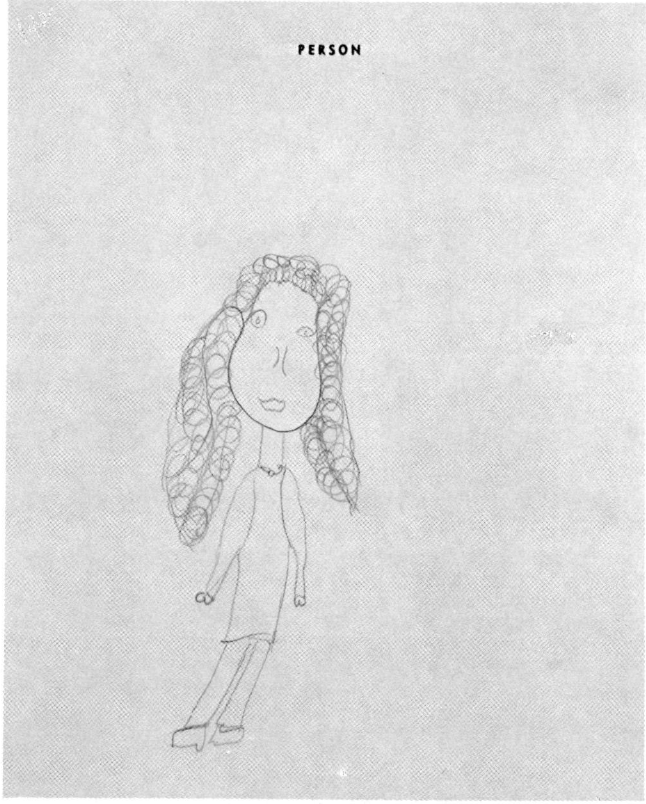

Plate 143

## Hair, Darkly Shaded

1. Uneasiness over fantasy life (Mogar, 1962)
2. Excessive sexuality or sensuality as occasionally seen in adolescents (Urban, 1963)

Also Illustrated

(a) Shoulders, squared (Plate 172)
(b) Hands, omitted (Plate 149)

**Hair, Darkly Shaded** Plate 143

PERSON
10

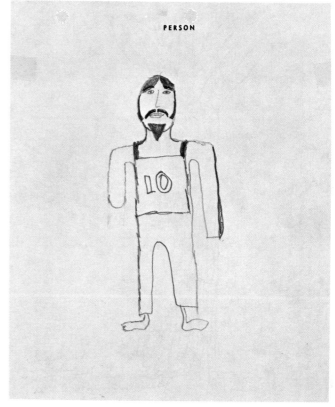

Plate 144 **Hair, Long and Unshaded**

PERSON

**Hair, Unshaded and Enclosing
Face in Vise-like Style**

Plate 145

PERSON

Plate 144

**Hair, Long and Unshaded**

Ambivalent fantasies regarding sexual matters (Buck, 1966)

Also Illustrated

(a) Fingers, short and rounded (Plate 142)
(b) Knees, emphasized (Plate 157)
(c) Shoulders, unusually small (Plate 174)
(d) Feet, unusually small (Plate 137)

Plate 145

**Hair, Unshaded and Enclosing
Face in Vise-like Style**

Feeling of being controlled by hostile feelings (Jolles, 1971)

Also Illustrated

(a) Legs, unusually long (Plate 159)
(b) Arms, unusually long (Plate 116)
(c) Eyes, hollow and empty (Plate 130)
(d) Nose, emphasized (Plate 166)

## Plate 146

### Hands, Concealed in Pockets

1. Occasionally represents compulsive masturbatory activity (DiLeo, 1973)
2. Associated with loafing or delinquent behavior (McElhaney, 1969)

Also Illustrated

(a) Hair, darkly shaded (Plate 143)
(b) Details, numerous and painstakingly drawn (Plate 4)

**Hands, Concealed in Pockets**   Plate 146

PERSON

## Plate 147

### Hands, Covering Pelvic Region

1. Possible self-stimulatory practices (Hammer, 1965)
2. Fear of sexual advances in female drawings (Urban, 1963)

Also Illustrated

(a) Arms akimbo (Plate 110)
(b) Shoulders, large (Plate 173)
(c) Muscles, emphasized (Plate 162)

**Hands, Covering Pelvic Region**   Plate 147

PERSON

Plate 148      **Hands, Mitten-like**

PERSON

Plate 148

**Hands, Mitten-like**

1. Aggression, currently repressed or suppressed (Buck, 1950)
2. Possible regressive tendencies (McElhaney, 1963)

Also Illustrated

(a) Shoulders, unusually large (Plate 173)
(b) Lines, dark (Plate 8)

Plate 149      **Hands, Omitted**

PERSON

Plate 149

**Hands, Omitted**

1. Most frequently omitted feature of human drawings (Buck, 1948)
2. Feelings of inadequacy (Gilbert, 1969)
3. Possible castration feelings (Evans & Marmorston, 1963)
4. Shyness, withdrawal and depression in children (Koppitz, 1966)

Also Illustrated

(a) Mouth, unusually large (Plate 161)
(b) Hair, darkly shaded (Plate 143)

Plate 150

## Hands, Shaded

1. Anxiety (Koppitz, 1968)
2. Guilt feelings about aggression and/or masturbation (Levy, 1958)

Also Illustrated

(a) Lines, sketchy (Plate 11)
(b) Feet, Unusually small (Plate 137)
(c) Hair, darkly shaded (Plate 143)

**Hands, Shaded** Plate 150

PERSON

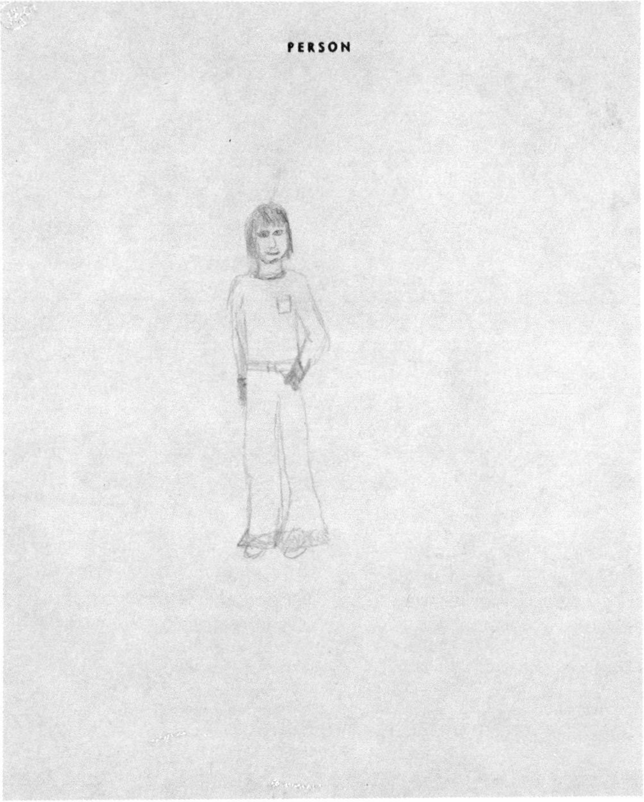

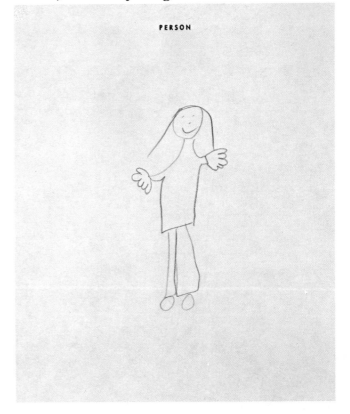

Plate 151

## Hands, Unusually Large

1. Need to compensate for feelings of inadequacy (Levy, 1958)
2. Possible impulsivity and social clumsiness (Buck, 1966)

Also Illustrated

(a) Shoulders, omitted (Plate 171)
(b) Neck, long and thin (Plate 163)
(c) Arms, short (Plate 119)

**Hands, Unusually Large** Plate 151

PERSON

Plate 152 **Hands, Unusually Small**

PERSON

Plate 152

## Hands, Unusually Small

1. Insecurity (DiLeo, 1973)
2. Helplessness (Hammer, 1954)

Also Illustrated

(a) Trunk, long and narrow (Plate 179)
(b) Feet, unusually small (Plate 137)
(c) Head, unusually large (Plate 155)

Plate 153 **Head, with Irregular Contour**

PERSON

Plate 153

## Head, with Irregular Contour

1. Organicity (Schildkrout *et al.,* 1973)
2. Possible psychosis (Machover, 1949)

Also Illustrated

(a) Hands, omitted (Plate 149)
(b) Ears, emphasized (Plate 129)

# Person

## Plate 154

### Head, Not Aligned or "Floating"

Possible Brain damage (Jordan, 1970)

Also Illustrated

(a) Hair, darkly shaded (Plate 143)
(b) Arms, held rigidly to body (Plate 118)

## Plate 155

### Head, Unusually Large

1. Grandiose ego-expansive tendencies (Levy, 1958)
2. If very large, paranoia and narcissism are suggested (Machover, 1951)
3. Overevaluation placed upon intelligence or high intellectual aspirations (Levy, 1958)
4. Fantasy is basic source of satisfaction (Urban, 1965)

Also Illustrated

(a) Mouth, unusually large (Plate 161)
(b) Eyes, unusually large or reinforced (Plate 132)

**Head, Unusually Large**     Plate 155

Plate 156      **Head, Unusually Small**

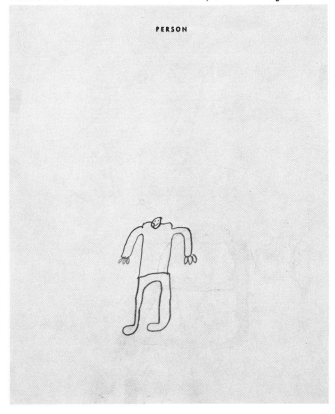

Plate 156

### Head, Unusually Small

1. Inadequate or impotent feelings (Machover, 1949)
2. Feelings of intellectual inferiority (Urban, 1963)
3. Ego structure weak (Machover, 1949)

Also Illustrated

(a) Lines, dark (Plate 8)
(b) Shoulders, squared (Plate 172)

Plate 157      **Knees, Emphasized**

Plate 157

### Knees, Emphasized

1. Possible homosexual inclinations (Schildkrout *et al.,* 1972)
2. Knee caps drawn suggest possible paranoid tendencies (McElhaney, 1969)

Also Illustrated

(a) Stance, broad (Plate 175)
(b) Arms, akimbo (Plate 110)

**Person**

## Plate 158

### Legs, Rigidly Held Together

1. Rigidity and possible sexual maladjustment (Buck, 1950)
2. With small shaded figures, repressive, self-conscious and apprehensive conditions suggested (Machover, 1949)
3. In a female's drawing of a female, fear of or subconscious desire for sexual advance (Machover, 1949)

Also Illustrated

(a) Chin, prominent (Plate 126)
(b) Lines, sketchy (Plate 11)

**Legs, Rigidly Held Together**     Plate 158

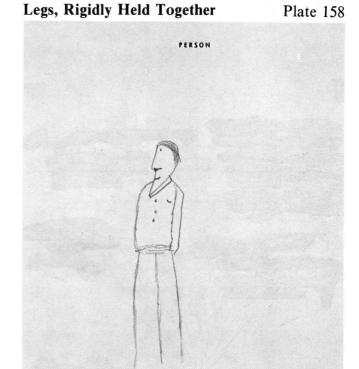

## Plate 159

### Legs, Unusually Long

1. Strong need for autonomy (Hammer, 1954)
2. Need to rise above environmental constrictions (Jolles, 1971)

Also Illustrated

(a) Shading, excessive (Plate 23)
(b) Details, atypical (Plate 2)

**Legs, Unusually Long**     Plate 159

Plate 160        **Legs, Unusually Short**

Plate 160

### Legs, Unusually Short

1. Feelings of physiological and/or psychological immobility (Buck, 1950)
2. Feelings of environmental constriction (Urban, 1963)

Also Illustrated

(a) Hair, darkly shaded (Plate 143)
(b) Lines, dark (Plate 8)

Plate 161        **Mouth, Unusually Large**

Plate 161

### Mouth, Unusually Large

1. Oral eroticism or verbal aggressiveness associated with dependence (Halpern, 1965)
2. Regressive personality (Gurvitz, 1951)
3. In children, normal dependency indicated, (Urban, 1963)

Also Illustrated

(a) Eyes, unusually large or reinforced (Plate 132)
(b) Feet, unusually long (Plate 136)
(c) Buttons, emphasized or numerous (Plate 125)

# Person

## Plate 162

### Muscles, Overly Emphasized

1. Body narcissism (Jolles, 1971)
2. By self-absorbed individuals, possible schizoid tendencies (Machover, 1949)

Also Illustrated

(a) Head, unusually small (Plate 156)
(b) Shoulders, unusually large (Plate 173)

**Muscles, Overly Emphasized**   Plate 162

PERSON

## Plate 163

### Neck, Long and Thin

1. Schizoid tendencies (Buck, 1969)
2. Hysteria in neurotic individuals (Levy, 1958)
3. Feelings of body weakness or inferiority (Urban, 1963)

Also Illustrated

(a) Eyes, unusually large or reinforced (Plate 132)
(b) Ears, emphasized (Plate 129)

**Neck, Long and Thin**   Plate 163

PERSON

Plate 164                              **Neck, Omitted**

PERSON

Plate 164

**Neck, Omitted**

1. Impulsivity in adolescents and adults (Mundy, 1972)
2. Immaturity as seen in the mentally defective (Mundy, 1972)
3. Possible organicity in adolescents and adults (Koppitz, 1968)

Also Illustrated

(a) Buttons, emphasized or numerous (Plate 125)
(b) Feet, unusually long (Plate 136)

Plate 165                         **Neck, Short and Thick**

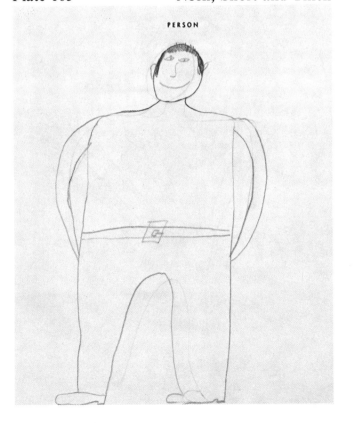

PERSON

Plate 165

**Neck, Short and Thick**

1. Gruff and stubborn tendencies (Urban, 1963)
2. Impulsivity (Machover, 1949)

Also Illustrated

(a) Trunk, unusually large (Plate 181)
(b) Hair, darkly shaded (Plate 143)

# Person

## Plate 166

### Nose, Emphasized

1. Phallic preoccupation and/or castration fears (Hammer, 1954)
2. Sexual inadequacy with compensatory feelings (Levy, 1958)
3. Possible homosexual tendencies (DiLeo, 1973)

Also Illustrated

(a) Profile, complete (Plate 169)
(b) Trunk, long and narrow (Plate 179)

Nose, Emphasized          Plate 166

## Plate 167

### Person, Running Blindly

At times may experience panic states (Jolles, 1971)

Also Illustrated

(a) Paper chopped drawing (Plate 16)
(b) Profile, ambivilent (Plate 170)

**Person, Running Blindly**     Plate 167

**Plate 168**

**Person, Running in Controlled Situation**

PERSON

**Plate 168**

**Person, Running in Controlled Situation**

Need to escape or heightened achievement needs (Jolles, 1971)

Also Illustrated

(a) Shading, excessive (Plate 23)
(b) Lines, dark (Plate 8)

**Plate 169**

**Profile, Complete**

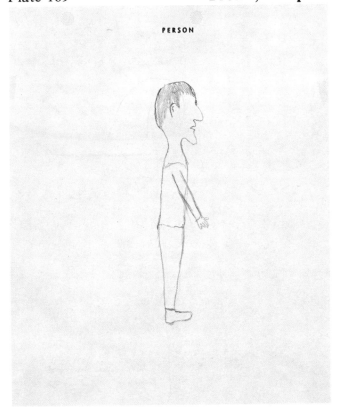

PERSON

**Plate 169**

**Profile, Complete**

1. Reluctance to face others; evasive (Buck, 1969)
2. Possible maladjustive withdrawal (Exner, 1962)
3. Interpersonal relationships tend to be reserved (Buck, 1950)

Also Illustrated

(a) Chin, prominent (Plate 126)
(b) Lines, sketchy (Plate 11)

**Person**

## Plate 170

### Profile, Ambivalent

1. Uneasy in social situations (Urban, 1963)
2. Guilt feelings; possible dishonesty (Machover, 1949)

Also Illustrated

(a) Chin, prominent (Plate 126)
(b) Transparent drawing (Plate 27)

**Profile, Ambivalent**   Plate 170

## Plate 171

### Shoulders, Omitted

1. Possible schizophrenia (Burton and Sjoberg, 1964)
2. Brain damaged conditions (Holzberg & Wexler, 1950)

Also Illustrated

(a) Groundline, darkly drawn (Plate 5)
(b) Sun (Plate 26)
(c) Hands, omitted (Plate 149)

**Shoulders, Omitted**   Plate 171

Plate 172       **Shoulders, Squared**       Plate 172

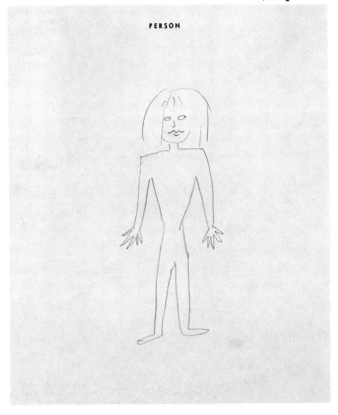

PERSON

**Shoulders, Squared**

1. Aggression, hostile tendencies (Goldstein & Rawn, 1957)
2. Defensive attitude (Hammer, 1965)

Also Illustrated

(a) Fingers, long and spike-like (Plate 138)
(b) Eyes, pupils omitted (Plate 131)

Plate 173       **Shoulders, Unusually Large**       Plate 173

PERSON

**Shoulders, Unusually Large**

1. Overconcern about need for strength or power; insecurity (Hammer, 1958)
2. Females drawn with broad shoulders by males and males drawn with large bosom-like shoulders suggest confusion over sex roles (Machover, 1949)

Also Illustrated

(a) Legs, short (Plate 160)
(b) Belt, darkly shaded (Plate 122)

# Person

## Plate 174

### Shoulders, Unusually Small

Inferiority feelings (Urban, 1963)

Also Illustrated

(a) Eyes, pupils omitted (Plate 131)
(b) Mouth, unusually large (Plate 161)

**Shoulders, Unusually Small**    Plate 174

## Plate 175

### Stance, Broad

1. Possible acting-out tendencies spawned by defiance of authority and/or insecurity (Hammer, 1969)
2. When in middle of page possible assertive potential (Shneidman, 1958)

Also Illustrated

(a) Fingers, short and rounded (Plate 142)
(b) Shoulders, unusually large (Plate 173)

**Stance, Broad**    Plate 175

Plate 176       **Stance, on Tiptoe**

PERSON

Plate 176

**Stance, on Tiptoe**

1. Reality grasp is tenuous (Hammer, 1954)
2. Need for flight (Urban, 1963)

Also Illustrated

(a) Breasts, emphasized (Plate 123)
(b) Lines, sketchy (Plate 11)

Plate 177       **Stance, Slanted, with Legs Floating**

PERSON

Plate 177

**Stance, Slanted, with Legs Floating**

1. Insecurity with dependency (Deabler, 1969)
2. In children, adjustive reaction is poor with impulsive aggressiveness (Koppitz, 1968)

Also Illustrated

(a) Hair, darkly shaded (Plate 143)
(b) Eyes, pupils omitted (Plate 131)

Plate 178

## Teeth, Prominently Displayed

1. Aggression or sadistic tendencies (Halpern, 1965)
2. Frequently seen in drawings of schizophrenics, hysterics and mental defectives, though occasionally in drawings of aggressive normals (Hammer, 1965)

Also Illustrated

(a) Buttons, emphasized or numerous (Plate 125)
(b) Arms, overly long (Plate 116)

**Teeth, Prominently Displayed** Plate 178

PERSON

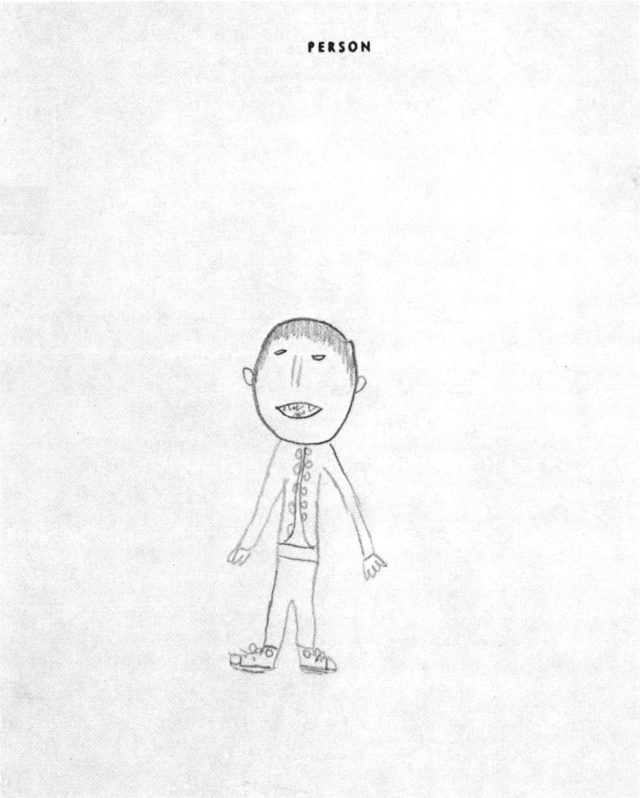

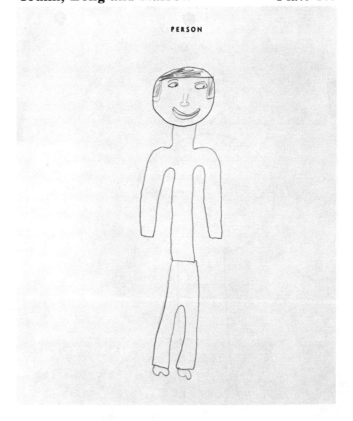

Plate 179

## Trunk, Long and Narrow

Possible schizoid tendencies (Urban, 1963)

Also Illustrated

(a) Hands, omitted (Plate 149)
(b) Legs, short (Plate 160)

**Trunk, Long and Narrow** Plate 179

PERSON

Plate 180        **Trunk, Omitted**

Trunk, Large;
**Waist Emphasized**

Plate 181

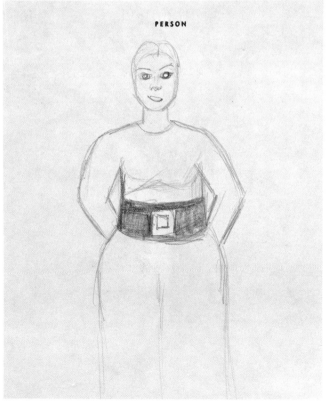

Plate 180

### Trunk, Omitted

1. Organicity or mental retardation (Mundy, 1972)
2. Adjustment to school is poor (Koppitz, 1968)
3. Denial of body drives (Jolles, 1971)

Also Illustrated

(a) Hair, darkly shaded (Plate 143)
(b) Head, unusually large (Plate 155)

Plate 181

### Trunk, Large;
### Waist Emphasized

1. Heightened awareness of unsatisfied motives or drives (Buck, 1950)
2. Sexual conflict (Hammer, 1954)

Also Illustrated

(a) Paper-chopped drawing (Plate 16)
(b) Belt, darkly shaded (Plate 122)

Plate 182

## Trunk, Small and Tightened

1. Body drives denied (Buck, 1950)
2. Inferiority feelings (Urban, 1963)
3. Homosexual tendencies in males (Buck, 1966)

Also Illustrated

(a) Hair, long and unshaded (Plate 144)
(b) Legs, unusually long (Plate 159)

**Trunk, Small and Tightened** Plate 182

PERSON

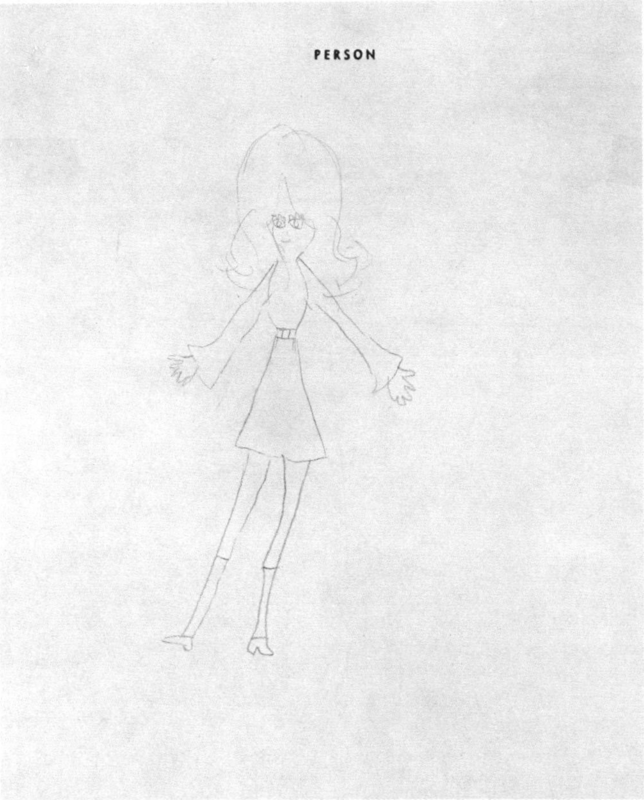

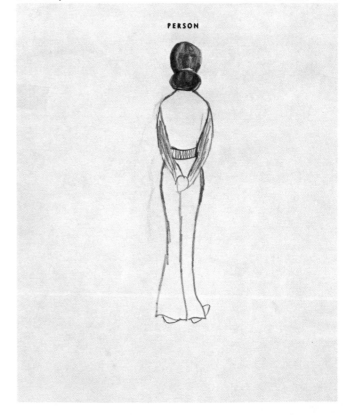

Plate 183

## Trunk, Reversed

1. Withdrawal from social contact (Buck, 1948)
2. Psychosis (Buck, 1966)

Also Illustrated

(a) Hair, darkly shaded (Plate 143)
(b) Belt, darkly shaded (Plate 122)

**Trunk, Reversed** Plate 183

PERSON

# IX. Non-Illustrated Characteristics with Interpretations

(Characteristics are alphabetized within the categories of General, House, Tree, and Person respectively.)

## General

DETAILS, LABELED
Possible psychosis (McElhaney, 1969)

DISTORTIONS, MODERATE
Anxiety (Handler & Reyher, 1965)

DISTORTIONS, SEVERE
1. Psychoses characterized by poor reality orientation (Burton & Sjoberg, 1964); mental retardation (McElhaney, 1969); or possible organicity (Small, 1973)
2. In adolescents, low self-esteem (Bodwin & Brick, 1960), perhaps with emotional disturbance (Hiler & Nesvig, 1965)
3. In children, situational stress for otherwise normals (Britain, 1970); unsatisfactory personal & school adjustment (Koppitz, 1966)

ERASURES, NUMEROUS
1. Indecisive and restless personality with felt uncertainty (Schildkrout et al., 1972)
2. Anxiety suggested (Jacks, 1969)

FATIGUE, NOTICEABLE
Depression of mood tone with reduction of efficiency (Jolles, 1971)

GROUNDLINE, DRAWN SPONTANEOUSLY
1. Feelings of insecurity (Buck, 1950)
2. Need for steadiness (Jolles, 1964)

LINES, FAINTLY DRAWN FOR SELECTED DETAIL
Apprehension by subject to deal with symbol in question (Jolles, 1971).

LINES, STEADY
1. Satisfactory adjustment (Levy, 1958)
2. Tenacity and high aspirations (Levy, 1958)

MOUNTAINS, SPONTANEOUSLY DRAWN
Dependency, often maternal in nature; defensive attitudes (Jolles, 1971).

MOVEMENT, DIRECTIONAL EMPHASIS UPON
1. If horizontal, timidity and self-protection (Alschuler & Hattwick, 1947)
2. If vertical, forcefulness and determination (Levy, 1958)
3. If continually changing, insecurity (Wolff, 1946)

MUTILATION OF DRAWING
Hostility, aggression (Jacks, 1969)

PERSEVERATION
Possible organicity (Burgemeister, 1962)

PLACEMENT, AT LEFT
1. Impulsivity, difficulty in delaying gratification of needs (Bradfield, 1964)
2. Tendency toward extroversion (Hammer, 1969); may indicate overconcern with self (Urban, 1963)

PLACEMENT, AT RIGHT
1. Behavior is realistic, controlled, and reasonably stable (Marzolf & Kirchner, 1972)
2. Possible use of intellect to control emotions (Buck, 1950)

PLACEMENT, BOTTOM CORNER
Inferiority feelings, possibly at an abnormal level (McElhaney, 1969)

PLACEMENT, BOTTOM LEFT CORNER
Depressive tendencies, with longing to return to conditions of the past (Buck, 1948)

PLACEMENT, CENTRAL
1. Normality; relative security (Lakin, 1956)
2. If exactly in center, suggests lack of flexibility in interpersonal relationships as well as insecurity (Buck, 1948)

PLACEMENT, CORNER (ANY)
Possible tendency to withdraw (Hammer, 1958)

PLACEMENT, HIGH
1. High level of energy, or defenses compensating for low drive level (Machover, 1949)
2. Goal-oriented, ambitious individual (Urban, 1963)

PLACEMENT, LOW
1. Feelings of inadequacy or insecurity (DiLeo, 1973)
2. Tendency toward depression, possibly with attitude of submission (Halpern, 1965)

PLACEMENT, TOP LEFT CORNER
1. Suggests regression (Barnouw, 1969)
2. Indicative of an insecure, withdrawn, fearful individual who tends to fantasize (Levine & Sapolsky, 1969)

PLACEMENT, TOP RIGHT CORNER
1. Repression of past events viewed as unacceptable (Buck, 1948)
2. Inappropriately optimistic expectations for future (Buck, 1948)

PRESSURE, CONSTANT
1. Normal, satisfactory adjustment (Urban, 1963)
2. If unusually unvaried and if suggested by corroborative evidence, possible catatonia (Hammer, 1958)

PRESSURE, UNUSUALLY HEAVY
1. Extreme anxiety (Kadis, 1950)
2. Organicity (Payne, 1948)
3. Indication of high drive level (Hetherington, 1952) or of forceful individuals with high ambitions (Alschuler & Hattwick, 1947)

PRESSURE, UNUSUALLY INCONSISTENT
1. If drawings normal otherwise, flexibility and ability to adapt to new situations (Hammer, 1958)
2. Variable drive level (Machover, 1949)

PRESSURE, UNUSUALLY LIGHT
1. Insecurity, timidity, and indecisiveness (Rosenzweig & Kogan, 1949); unsatisfactory adjustment with decreased ego strength (Buck, 1969)
2. Low drive levels (Precker, 1950)
3. In children, low level of energy (Kadis, 1950) or strongly controlled personality, possibly with considerable repression (Alschuler & Hattwick, 1947)

SHADING, ABSENCE OF
Possible character disorder (Deabler, 1969)

SIZE, EXTREMELY SMALL
Possible schizophrenia (Kahn & Giffen, 1960)

SIZE, UNUSUALLY LARGE
1. Tendency to act-out aggressive feelings (Zimmerman & Garfinkle, 1942)
2. Use of repression and other defenses to compensate for feelings of inadequacy (Wysocki & Whitney, 1965)

SIZE, UNUSUALLY SMALL
1. Low self-concept (Mundy, 1972)
2. Anxiety (Waehner, 1946)
3. Withdrawal tendencies (Gilbert, 1969)

TURNING PAPER WHILE DRAWING

Negativistic tendencies (Hammer, 1954)

WIND

Subject feels at mercy of pressures over which he has little control (Jolles, 1971)

# House

ANGULATION, FAULTY PRODUCTION OF

Possible organicity (Deabler, 1969)

BATHROOM

Focus upon elimination and sanitation (Jolles, 1971)

BLUEPRINTS

1. Severe domestic conflict (Buck, 1948)
2. If well done, possible tendencies toward paranoia; if of very poor quality, possible organicity (Jacks, 1969)

CHIMNEY, EASILY DRAWN

Normal stable adjustment (Buck, 1966)

CHIMNEY, MORE THAN ONE

1. Above average interest with sexual matters (Jolles, 1964); possible compensation for sexual inadequacy (Hammer, 1954)
2. Anxiety concerning interpersonal intimacy (Jolles, 1952)

CHIMNEY, TWO-DIMENSIONAL

By males, feelings of inadequacy sexually (Levine & Sapolsky, 1969)

CLOSE VIEW

1. Warmth felt in interpersonal relationships (Jolles, 1952)
2. Psychological openness (Jolles, 1964)

DISTANT VIEW

1. Withdrawal tendencies; inaccessibility (Buck, 1950)
2. Feeling that domestic difficulties are overwhelming (Hammer, 1958)

DOOR, DRAWN LAST

1. Desire to avoid interpersonal relationships (Buck, 1948)
2. Withdrawal (Buck, 1966)

DOOR, OPEN

Significant need to use environment to obtain emotional support; if house is vacant, suggests absence of ego defense (Barnouw, 1969)

DOOR, WITH HEAVY LOCK AND/OR HINGES

1. Noticeable defensiveness, with withdrawal (Hammer, 1958)
2. Distrust of others, perhaps hostile (Buck, 1948)

HOUSE, CONSISTING ONLY OF ROOF (NOT A-FRAME)

1. Excessive use of fantasy (Buck, 1950)
2. Possible psychotic episode (Deabler, 1969)

HOUSE, ON VERGE OF COLLAPSE

Possible incipient psychosis (Hammer, 1969)

HOUSE, REAR-VIEW PRESENTATION

1. Negativism (Jolles, 1964)
2. Tendency to withdraw (Jolles, 1964)

OUTHOUSE

1. Hostile aggression (Buck, 1966)
2. Possible character disorder (Deabler, 1969)

PERSPECTIVE, SINGLE (ONE WALL)

1. Strong need to present appropriate interpersonal facade (Buck, 1950)

2. In children younger than eight years of age, normality (Jolles, 1952)

PILLARS, UNUSUALLY HIGH

Reality contact questionable; possible organicity (Jolles, 1971)

ROOF, SHADING OF

1. Anxiety (Buck, 1969)
2. Use of fantasy (Jolles, 1971)

ROOF, WITH INCOMPLETE CLOSURE OF APEX

1. Poor reality contact (Levine & Sapolsky, 1969)
2. Ego boundaries not firmly established; may be pathological (Landisberg, 1969)

SHADES, EXTENSION BEYOND WINDOWS

Possible psychosis (Hammer, 1969)

SHUTTERS

1. If open, indication of receptiveness and potential for meaningful interpersonal relationships (Hammer, 1954)
2. If closed, sign of extremely withdrawn individual, possibly pathologically defensive (Jolles, 1964)

SIDEWALK

1. If easily and appropriately drawn, satisfactory adjustment and ease in relating to others (Marzolf & Kirchner, 1972)
2. If very long, difficulty in socialization, with felt need to improve skills in this area (Buck, 1950)
3. If wide at end, becoming progressively narrow toward house, surface attitude of friendliness, with inner desire to maintain psychological distance (Hammer, 1958)
4. If broad, sign of social accessibility (Hammer, 1954)

SIZE, FULL-PAGE

1. Feeling that one's environment is constrictive, with considerable amount of resultant frustration (Buck, 1948)
2. Defensive use of fantasy or overcompensation (Buck, 1950)

SIZE, TINY

1. Tendency to withdraw (Buck, 1948)
2. Feelings of inadequacy (Buck, 1950)

SMOKE, WITHOUT CHIMNEY

Lack of sexual desires (Hammer, 1969)

WALLS, INCOMPLETE CONNECTION OF

1. Feeling that primitive drives are overwhelming, perhaps with feelings of depersonalization (Jolles, 1964)
2. Possibility of organicity (Jolles, 1952)

WINDOWS, APPROPRIATE NUMBER AND SIZE OF

Normalcy (Hammer, 1954)

WINDOWS, FEW

Possibility of regression (Meyer, et al., 1955)

WINDOWS, HEAVY REINFORCEMENT OF

1. Anxiety regarding relationships with others (Buck, 1950)
2. Possible orificial fixations, with concomitant anxiety (Levine & Sapolsky, 1969)

WINDOWS, MANY

1. Possible tendency to display sexuality, especially if in bedroom (Buck, 1948)
2. If with shades, anxiety concerning interaction with environment (Buck, 1966)

WINDOWS, OPEN

1. Inadequate ego control (Jolles, 1952)
2. Difficulties in adjustment, due to oral fixations (Levine & Sapolsky, 1969)

WINDOWS, OVAL

In women, liberal nonconformist attitudes (Marzolf & Kirchner, 1972)

WINDOWS, TRIANGULAR

Preoccupation with female sex symbol (Jolles, 1964)

WINDOWS, UNUSUALLY SMALL

1. Inaccessibility psychologically (Jolles, 1952)
2. Disinterest in interpersonal relationships (Buck, 1948)

WINDOWS, WITH BARRED APPEARANCE (INTERSTICES, ETC.)

Feeling that room represented is place of imprisonment (Buck, 1966)

WINDOWS, WITH LOCKS EMPHASIZED

Excessive defensiveness (Buck, 1966)

# Tree

BARK, EASILY AND APPROPRIATELY DRAWN

Normality (Buck, 1966)

BRANCH, SINGLE (TWO-DIMENSIONAL) ON TWO-DIMENSIONAL TRUNK

Traumatic experience(s) following satisfactory early emotional development (Jolles, 1964)

BRANCHES, DETACHED FROM TRUNK

Inadequate ability to deal with environment (Mursell, 1969)

BRANCHES, EXTENDING BEYOND TOP OF PAPER

1. Emphasis on satisfaction of fantasies (Buck, 1950)
2. Impulsivity (Levine & Sapolsky, 1969)

BRANCHES, FALLING

Possible decreased ability to withstand pressure from environment (Buck, 1966)

BRANCHES, LONG, THIN, AND POINTING UPWARD, NOT OUTWARD

1. Excessive fantasy, often seen in schizoid individuals (Hammer, 1958)
2. Fear of reaching out to environment for need satisfaction (Jolles, 1952)

BRANCHES, NEGLIGENT TREATMENT OF

1. Unpleasant interpersonal relationships (Hammer, 1953)
2. Unsatisfactory interpersonal interactions (Hammer, 1953)

BRANCH, ON LOWER PART OF TRUNK

Regressive tendencies (Koch, 1952)

BRANCHES, SHORT AND BLEAK

Perception of environment as unhappy (Koch, 1952)

BRANCHES, THICKER AT EXTREMITIES

Possible aggression (Koch, 1952)

BRANCHES, VERY LIGHTLY DRAWN

Indication of anxious, indecisive behavior (Buck, 1948)

BRANCHES, WIDE, SHORT AND APPEARING "CUT-OFF"

Possible suicidal tendencies (Brown, 1958)

CHRISTMAS TREE

Sign of dependency; much weaker indicator if drawn during Christmas season (Hammer, 1954)

CROWN, SACK-LIKE, HIDING LARGE PART OF TRUNK

Passive indecision (Koch, 1952)

DOG, URINATING ON TREE

Character disorder of aggressive nature (Deabler, 1969)

LEAVES, NOT CONNECTED TO BRANCHES

1. Possibly decompensation (Levine & Sapolsky, 1969)

2. If many, an obsessive-compulsive individual (Levine & Sapolsky, 1969)

LEAVES, NUMEROUS

Feigned productivity, with possible obsessive-compulsive tendencies (Levine & Sapolsky, 1969)

LEAVES, OMISSION OF

1. Psychologically barren individual; inadequate ego integration (Levine & Sapolsky, 1969)
2. Of less interpretive consequence if drawn during winter (Judson & McCasland, 1960)

LEAVES, POINTED SHARPLY

Possible aggression and acting-out behavior (Jacks, 1969)

LEAVES, TWO-DIMENSIONAL AND DRAWN WITH EXCESSIVE CARE

Obsessive-compulsive tendencies (Buck, 1966)

LEAVES, TWO-DIMENSIONAL AND OVERLY LARGE IN PROPORTION TO BRANCHES

1. Feigned satisfactory adjustment; compensating for feelings of inadequacy (Buck, 1950)
2. Compensatory reality flight (Jolles, 1952)

LEFT BRANCHES EMPHASIZED

Impulsive acting-out behavior, suggestive of personality imbalance (Buck, 1966)

RIGHT BRANCHES EMPHASIZED

Frequent avoidance or postponement of emotional satisfaction (Jolles, 1964)

ROOTS, DEAD

Conscious lack of contact with reality (Buck, 1950)

ROOTS, INADEQUATE ORGANIZATION OF

Unstable, inadequate personality (Buck, 1948)

ROOTS, OMITTED, WITHOUT BASELINE

Inadequacy feelings; insecurity (Michal-Smith & Morgenstern, 1969)

ROOTS, OVEREMPHASIZED AS THEY ENTER GROUND

Struggle to maintain contact with reality (Hammer, 1954)

ROOTS, SHADED

Anxious, insecure individual (Michael-Smith & Morgenstern, 1969)

ROOTS, TAPERING SMOOTHLY INTO GROUND

Appropriate reality orientation (Buck, 1966)

ROOTS, THIN AND POOR CONTACT WITH GROUND

Inadequate grasp of reality (Mursell, 1969)

SAPLING

1. Immaturity (Buck, 1948)
2. Regressive tendencies (Meyer et al., 1955)

SCAR, ON TRUNK

Representation of trauma (Levine & Galanter, 1953)

SWING IN TREE

In women, anxiety-free state; liberal attitude with willingness to experiment (Marzolf & Kirchner, 1972)

TREE, ALONE ON HILL

1. Possible feelings of grandeur (Buck, 1950)
2. Difficulty in achieving autonomy (Hammer, 1954)

TREE, BLOWN BY WIND

Feeling that environment is in complete control of one's life; possible social overtones (Hammer, 1958)

TREE, DEAD

1. Severe emotional disturbance (Hammer, 1958)
2. Depression, guilt, extreme feelings of inadequacy (Barnouw, 1969)

TREE, DRAWN IN A DEPRESSION
Feelings of inadequacy and/or depression (Buck, 1950)

TREE, LARGE
Overconcern with self, most notably if tree is in center of page (Levine & Sapolsky, 1969)

TREE, LEANING TOWARD LEFT
1. Desire for immediate gratification of emotional needs or acting-out tendencies, with consequent personality imbalance (Buck, 1950)
2. Fear of future, with or without fixations of the past (Jolles, 1952)

TREE, LEANING TOWARD RIGHT
1. Emotional impulsivity feared by individual, with consequent personality imbalance (Koch, 1952)
2. Repression of unpleasant past, or inappropriate optimism concerning future (Buck, 1948)

TREE, ON SIDE OF HILL
1. Struggle to achieve goals (Buck, 1966)
2. Insecurity and need to seek shelter (Jolles, 1964)

TREE, TINY
Somewhat withdrawn individual with feelings of inadequacy (Buck, 1948)

TREE, VERY LARGE
1. Aggressive tendencies (Buck, 1948)
2. Overcompensatory behavior and/or use of fantasy (Buck, 1950)

TRUNK, BROAD WITH BROAD BASE
1. Tendency toward oral dependency (Levine & Sapolsky, 1969)
2. Drawn by inhibited individuals or those of subnormal intelligence (Koch, 1952)

TRUNK, DEAD
Feeling that one has lost ability to control gratification of impulses (Buck, 1950)

TRUNK, HUGE THOUGH NOT NECESSARILY BROAD-BASED
Feeling that environment imposes unnecessary limitations (Buck, 1950)

TRUNK, LONG WITH SMALL CROWN
Infantilism, retarded developmentally, or regressive tendencies in neurotics (Koch, 1952)

TRUNK, NEARLY BARE, WITH SMALL BRANCHES BEGINNING TO GROW
Spurt of emotional growth of recent origin; prior problems in psychological development (Hammer, 1958)

TRUNK, OUTER EDGES DARKLY DRAWN
Conscious need to maintain psychological stability (Hammer, 1954)

TRUNK, OUTLINE NOT CONTINUOUS
Excitable individual with impulsivity suggested (Koch, 1952)

TRUNK, SHADED, ESPECIALLY IF DEEP
1. Feelings of inferiority (Buck, 1948)
2. Perhaps psychosomatic conditions (Levine & Sapolsky, 1969)

TRUNK, SHORT, WITH LARGE CROWN
Ambitious, self-confident individual (Koch, 1952)

TRUNK, VERY LIGHTLY DRAWN
1. Weak ego strength (Buck, 1966)
2. Difficulty in making decisions (Jolles, 1964)

TRUNK, VERY SMALL AND SLENDER
Inadequate ego strength (Landisberg, 1969)

TRUNK, WITH THICKENED OR CONSTRICTED AREAS
Inhibited, possibly regressive, behavior (Koch, 1952)

WEEPING WILLOW TREE
Possibility of depression (Hammer, 1969)

# Person

ADAM'S APPLE, EMPHASIS OF
By males, sexual weakness (Machover, 1949)

ANGULAR FIGURE
Generally masculine orientation (Machover, 1949)

ARMS, DETACHED FROM TRUNK
1. Possible fear of castration (Hammer, 1953)
2. Feelings of inferiority (McElhaney, 1969)

ARMS, EXTENDED MECHANICALLY AND PERPENDICULAR TO BODY
1. Possible regression and unenthusiastic environmental contact (Machover, 1949)
2. By children, possible brain damage (Koppitz, 1968)

ARMS, FOLDED
1. Suspiciousness, with possible hostility (Buck, 1950)
2. Possible rigid attempts to control impulsive behavior (Urban, 1963)

ARMS, OMITTED
1. Feelings of guilt and inadequacy; indication of withdrawal (Kokonis, 1972)
2. If in drawing of opposite sex, possible feeling of heterosexual rejection (Machover, 1949)

ARMS, OMITTED IN OPPOSITE SEX DRAWING
Possible feelings of rejection by opposite sex, perhaps parent (Machover, 1949)

ARMS, ONE LONGER THAN OTHER
Anxiety regarding manual activities (Gurvitz, 1951)

ARMS, OUTSTRETCHED
Desire for interaction with environment and/or other people (Michal-Smith & Morgenstern, 1969)

ARMS, REINFORCEMENT OF
Excessive striving, usually for physical achievements (Shneidman, 1958)

ARMS, TRANSPARENT
Possible feelings of inadequacy (Buck, 1969)

BELT BUCKLE, EMPHASIS OF
Dependent tendencies (Machover, 1951)

BREASTS, OMISSION OF
1. By females, feelings of immaturity (Brown, 1958), or uncharitable feelings toward children (Machover, 1949)
2. Possibility of schizophrenia (Burton & Sjoberg, 1964)

BREASTS, VERY SMALL
1. Possibility of normality (Ries et al., 1966)
2. May feel rejected by mother (Machover, 1949)
3. By female, possible reluctance to give affection to children; fear that mature sexuality will be rejected (Urban, 1963)

CANE
1. Sex symbol; if emphasized, possible preoccupation with sex (Buck, 1950)
2. By male, possible homosexual tendencies (McElhaney, 1969)

CHILD OF SUBJECT'S SEX
By adults, possible regression (Meyer et al., 1955)

CIGARETTE
Sex symbol; if emphasized, possible preoccupation with sex (Buck, 1950)

CLOTHING, STRIPED
1. If horizontal, poor impulse control (Schildkrout et al., 1972)
2. If repetitious, possible compulsivity (Schildkrout *et al.,* 1972)

CLOWNS, WITCHES, AND SOLDIERS
1. Hostile and punitive tendencies, perhaps of delinquent nature (Urban, 1963)
2. Possibility that subject is resistive toward testing situation, especially if clown is drawn (Urban, 1963)
3. If witch is drawn, hostile feelings toward females are suggested (Jolles, 1964)

COWBOYS
1. Possibility of masculine needs; immature tendencies (Hammer, 1958)
2. By adolescents, possibility of character disorder, perhaps with delinquency (Deabler, 1969)
3. By children, possibility of normality (Urban, 1963)

EARRINGS, EMPHASIS ON
1. Possibility of exhibitionistic tendencies (Levy, 1958) or paranoid feelings (McElhaney, 1969)
2. By male on female figure, suggestion of feminine attitudes (McElhaney, 1969)

EARS, AS QUESTION MARKS
Possible paranoid conditions (McElhaney, 1969)

EARS, WITH DARK DOTS IN AREA
Possibility of auditory hallucinations (Schildkrout *et al.,* 1972)

EYEBROWS, ELABORATE TREATMENT OF (ESPECIALLY IF ARCHED OR VERY TRIM)
1. Indication that uninhibited behavior is distasteful; possibility of overgrooming (Machover, 1949)
2. By males, effeminate tendencies (Urban, 1963)

EYEBROWS, FROWNING
Perhaps hostility (McElhaney, 1969)

EYEBROWS, RAISED
Possible contemptuous attitude (Urban, 1963)

EYEBROWS, THICK AND HEAVY
Tendency to be gruff (Machover, 1949)

EYELASHES, IN DETAIL
If by males, possible homosexual tendencies (DiLeo, 1973)

EYES, CLOSED
1. Repressed hostility (Schildkrout *et al.,* 1972)
2. In children over five, psychological disturbance (Koppitz, 1968)

EYES, OMISSION OF
1. Ineffective, undiscerning personality (Gurvitz, 1951)
2. Possible visual hallucinations (Buck, 1950) or schizophrenia (Deabler, 1969)
3. Possible voyeurism (Levy, 1950)

EYES, ON SIDE OF HEAD
Possibility of paranoid tendencies (Schildkrout *et al.,* 1972)

EYES, PERIPHERY REINFORCED
Possible paranoia (Reznikoff & Nicholas, 1958)

EYES, TWO DRAWN ON PROFILE
Possible schizophrenia (Gilbert, 1969)

EYES, WITH WIDE-EYED STARE
Possible hysteric conditions, (Schildkrout *et al.,* 1972)

FACE, SHADED
Indication of serious psychological disturbance, unless depiction of skin color, etc. (Koppitz, 1968)

FACIAL FEATURES, DISPLACED
Possibility of mental retardation (Hammer, 1969)

FACIAL FEATURES, FAINTLY DRAWN
1. Tendency to withdraw, most notably when in profile (Urban, 1963)
2. Interactions with others characterized by self-consciousness and shyness (Machover, 1949)

FACIAL FEATURES, NON-HUMAN OR OTHERWISE BIZARRE
Possible schizoid conditions (McElhaney, 1969)

FEET, BARE, ON CLOTHED FIGURE
Hostile, oppositional, and acting-out tendencies (Hammer, 1969)

FEET, EMPHASIZED
Difficulties in sexual matters (Hammer, 1954)

FEET, LARGE
Feelings of insecurity (Urban, 1963)

FEET, OMITTED
Feeling that environment is too limiting, with dependency (Evans & Marmorston, 1963)

FEET, POINTED DOWNWARD, IN V SHAPE
Possibility of involutional melancholia (Gilbert, 1969)

FEET, POINTED IN OPPOSITE DIRECTIONS
1. Indecisive regarding desire for independence (Urban, 1963)
2. Possible impulsivity (Schildkrout *et al.,* 1972)

FEET, SHARPLY POINTED
Possible hostility (Jacks, 1969)

FEET, VERY SMALL
Indication of need for security and dependence (Brown, 1958)

FEET, WITH EXCESSIVE DETAIL
Egocentric, possibly feminine, as well as obsessive tendencies (Jolles, 1964)

FEMALE FIGURE, APPEARING MASCULINE
By females, possible sign of masculine protest (Machover, 1949)

FEMALE FIGURE, APPEARING STRONGER
1. By males, possible difficulties in psychosexual adjustment; passive tendencies; or problems in sexual identification (Pollitt *et al.,* 1964)
2. By young boys, possible normality (Levy, 1958)

FEMALE FIGURE, CONSIDERABLY SMALLER THAN MALE
By males, possible virility strivings (Schildkrout *et al.,* 1972) or depression (Roback & Webersinn, 1966)

FEMALE FIGURE, FACELESS
By males, possible indication of hostile feelings toward females, or fear of relationships with females (Schildkrout, *et al.,* 1972)

FEMALE FIGURE, LACKING FEMININE CONTOURS
By females, possible frigidity (McElhaney, 1969)

FEMALE FIGURE, WITH LEGS EXPOSED, HAIR EMPHASIZED, AND BREASTS LARGE
By males, suggestion of strong sexual needs (Schildkrout *et al.,* 1972)

FIGURE, FRAGMENTATION OR DISORGANIZATION OF
1. Possible organicity or psychotic regression (Small, 1973)

2. In children under considerable pressure, possible normality (Britain, 1970)

FINGERNAILS, POINTED OR REINFORCED
Possible hostile feelings (Schildkrout et al., 1972)

FINGERS, FISTED
Possible rebellious behavior (Goldstein & Rawn, 1957)

FINGERS, JOINTS AND FINGERNAILS DETAILED
Tendency to be compulsive (Levy, 1958)

FINGERS, OMITTED
1. Problems in social effectiveness (Jolles, 1964)
2. Possible need to punish self for masturbation (Jolles, 1971)

FINGERS, TOO FEW
1. Indication of inadequacy feelings (Schildkrout et al., 1972)
2. By children, possible organicity (Koppitz, 1968)

FINGERS, TOO MANY
1. Possible ambition and aggression, with strong need for acquisition (Urban, 1963)
2. By children, possible organicity (Koppitz, 1968)

FINGERS, UNUSUALLY LARGE
Tendency to be assultive (Shneidman, 1958)

FINGERS, UNUSUALLY LONG
Individual with relatively dull personality who probably does not depend vocationally upon manual activity (Machover, 1949)

FINGERS, WITHOUT HANDS
1. By adults, possible regression, with tendencies to be aggressive in infantile manner (Machover, 1949)
2. Commonly drawn by children (Shneidman, 1958)

GENITALIA DRAWN
1. Pathological sign, perhaps indicative of schizophrenia (Kahn & Giffen, 1960)
2. Possible behavior disorder, perhaps psychopathy (Deabler, 1969)
3. Art students or individuals undergoing analysis (Machover, 1951)
4. By children, serious psychological disturbance and aggression (Koppitz, 1968)
5. By adolescents, possible curiosity and overconcern with sexual matters (Urban, 1963)
6. By the elderly, probable regression to primitive level (Wolk, 1969)

GUN
Sex symbol; if emphasized, possible preoccupation with sex (Buck, 1950)

HAIR, EMPHASIS UPON
1. Expression of virility strivings and overconcern with sexual matters (Gilbert, 1969)
2. Attempt to compensate for feelings of sexual inadequacy or impotency (Levy, 1950)

HAIR, IN DISARRAY
Confused thought processes (Levine & Sapolsky, 1969)

HAIR, OMITTED OR SPARSE
1. Feelings of sexual inadequacy (Buck, 1950)
2. Fear of castration (Hammer, 1953)

HANDS, DRAWN LAST
1. Inadequacy feelings (Urban, 1963)
2. Environmental contact perceived as undesirable or fearful (Urban, 1963)

HANDS, FAINTLY DRAWN
Sign of anxiety over social situations, perhaps due to lack of self-confidence (Machover, 1949)

HANDS, GLOVED
1. Possible difficulty in controlling emotionality (Machover, 1949)
2. Possible inhibition of aggressive feelings (Machover, 1949)

HANDS, HELD BEHIND BACK
1. Anxiety regarding manual activity (DiLeo, 1973)
2. Possibility of psychopathic tendencies (McElhaney, 1969)

HANDS, SWOLLEN
Possible inhibition of drives (Machover, 1955)

HAT, ON FIGURE
By female, possible venturesome tendencies (Marzolf & Kirchner, 1972)

HAT, PHALLIC
1. Possible fear of castration (Hammer, 1953)
2. If covering eyes, reluctance to interact with environment and other people (Machover, 1949)

HEAD, BACK VIEW
Withdrawal, possibly of the type seen in schizoid or paranoid conditions (Buck, 1966)

HEAD, LARGER ON ONE DRAWING
Sex depicted in that drawing is perceived as socially dominant by subject (Cook, 1951)

HEAD, DRAWN LAST
Indication of severe emotional disturbance (Machover, 1949)

HEAD, OMISSION OF
1. Fear of castration (Hammer, 1953)
2. Feel the need to repress unpleasant thoughts (Schildkrout et al., 1972)
3. Possibility of organicity (DiLeo, 1970)

HEAD, WITHOUT BODY
Possible schizophrenic condition (Baldwin, 1964)

HIPS AND BUTTOCKS, TWISTED AND EMPHASIZED ON MALE FIGURE
By males, possible homosexual tendencies (Geil, 1944)

HIPS, EMPHASIZED
1. By males, homosexual propensities (Levy, 1950)
2. By females, possible desire to bear children (Machover, 1951)

JOINTS, EMPHASIZED
1. Attempt to control feelings of bodily disorganization (Wildman, 1963)
2. Immature sexuality and dependence on mother (Levy, 1958)

LEGS AND FEET, DRAWN FIRST AND WITH MORE DETAIL
Feelings of discouragement, perhaps with guilt (Levy, 1950)

LEGS, CUT OFF BY BOTTOM OF PAPER
Individual may feel that autonomy has been lost (Buck, 1966)

LEGS, FEMININE, ON MALE FIGURE
Possible sex role confusion (Machover, 1949)

LEGS, MUSCULAR, ON FEMALE FIGURE
Possible sex role confusion (Machover, 1949)

LEGS, OF UNEQUAL SIZE
Poor adjustment concerning autonomy, sexuality, or independence (Buck, 1950)

LEGS, OMITTED

Feeling of being unable to move (Michal-Smith & Morgenstern, 1969)

LEGS, REINFORCEMENT OF

Possibility of aggression (Shneidman, 1958)

LEGS, WASTED IN APPEARANCE

Debilitating loss of autonomy (Reznikoff & Tomblen, 1956)

LIPS, FULL

Possibly narcissistic, sensual, or dependent individual (Machover, 1949)

LIPS, FULL, IN MALE FIGURE

By males, effeminate tendencies; if with lipstick, homosexual tendencies (Machover, 1949)

LIPS, PROTRUSION OF

Regressive oral tendencies (Meyer *et al.,* 1955)

MALE FIGURE GRANDIOSE, WITH STRONGER-APPEARING, PERHAPS SMALLER, FEMALE

By males, possible oppositional attitudes or desire to degrade females (Machover, 1949)

MALE FIGURE, OFF-BALANCE

By males, suggestion of inadequacy (McElhaney, 1969)

MALE FIGURE, WITH HEAVY SHADING

By females, possible anxiety concerning sexual activities (Schildkrout *et al.,* 1972)

MIDLINE, EMPHASIZED

Possible low self-esteem, accompanied by inferiority feelings (Bodwin & Bruck, 1960)

MOUTH, CONCAVE

1. Indication of oral passivity and infantile dependent behavior (Schildkrout *et al.,* 1972)
2. By children, possibility of normality (Machover, 1960)

MOUTH, CUPID BOW IN FEMALE FIGURES

1. By adolescent females, possible promiscuous behavior (Urban, 1963)
2. By adults, possibility of psychosomatic conditions (Urban, 1963)

MOUTH, DEPICTED AS SHORT, DARK LINE

Caution due to fear of retaliation for aggressive behavior (Machover, 1949)

MOUTH, DEPICTED AS SINGLE LINE, UNSMILING

1. Possible depression (McElhaney, 1969)
2. If in profile, strong anxiety (Machover, 1949)

MOUTH, DEPICTED AS SLASH LINE

Overly critical attitude; verbally aggressive behavior (Goldstein & Rawn, 1957)

MOUTH, GRINNING, DEPICTED BY WIDE UPTURNED LINE

1. In children, normality (Machover, 1949)
2. In adults, possible need to maintain facade of congeniality (Urban, 1963)

MOUTH, OBJECTS WITHIN

Possible oral eroticism (Urban, 1963)

MOUTH, OMISSION OF

1. Guilt regarding oral aggressive behavior (Machover, 1949)
2. Depression (Koppitz, 1966)

MOUTH, OPEN

Possible sign of oral passivity (Gurvitz, 1951)

MOUTH, VERY SMALL

Denial of oral dependency (Urban, 1963)

MOUTH, WITH SNEER

Hostility (McElhaney, 1969)

MOVEMENTS, NON-VIOLENT

Possible flexibility and normality; often associated with bright normal individuals (Jacks, 1969)

MOVEMENTS, VIOLENT

Possible aggression (Allen, 1958)

MOVEMENTS, WHIRLING

Possible schizophrenia (Schildkrout *et al.,* 1972)

NECK, ONE-DIMENSIONAL

1. Possible difficulties in maintaining cognitive control over body drives (Jolles, 1952)
2. Infantile impulsivity (Urban, 1963)

NECK, SHADING OF

By children over five, psychological disturbance (Koppitz, 1968)

NECK, VERY LONG

1. Problems in control of need satisfaction, partially due to poor coordination between intellect and emotions (Mursell, 1969)
2. Moralistic, socially conventional individuals (Machover, 1949)

NOSE, BUTTON

Immaturity, possibly infantile sexuality; suggestion of dependency (Urban, 1963)

NOSE, FAINT, SHADED, OR TRUNCATED

1. If by males, fear of castration, perhaps for autoeroticism (Hammer, 1953)
2. If by females, penis envy and hostile feelings toward males (Machover, 1949)

NOSE, OMISSION OF

1. If by children, emotional disturbance, often of withdrawal or depressive nature (Koppitz, 1966)
2. Perhaps feelings of castration (Schildkrout *et al.,* 1972)

NOSE, PHALLIC AND LONG

1. Possibility of exhibitionism (Hammer, 1969)
2. May be indication of loss of masculinity (Wolk, 1969)

NOSE, POINTED SHARPLY

Tendency to act-out (Hammer, 1965)

NOSE, TRIANGULAR

Immaturity, possibly infantile sexuality (Urban, 1963)

OPPOSITE SEX DRAWN FIRST

1. Possibility of ambivalent feelings or conflict concerning sex role; poor self-concept (Armon, 1960)
2. By female, of less interpretive consequence (Melikian & Wahab, 1969), but possible sexual identification problems (Armon, 1960) or competitive aggressive behavior (Heberlein & Marcuse, 1963)
3. By children, neurotic tendencies (McHugh, 1966)

OPPOSITE SEX DRAWN SMALLER, AND LESS ELABORATELY

1. Possible character disorder of narcissistic nature (Gilbert, 1969)
2. By children, female drawing is often larger (Weider & Noller, 1953); inconsistent presentations of male and female figures has been associated with anxiety and obsessions (Haworth, 1962)
3. By females, possible indication of strong strivings of masculine nature (Weider & Noller, 1953)

ORGANS, INTERNAL

Possible psychosis (Buck, 1966)

PERSON, APPEARING OLDER THAN SUBJECT

1. Possible parental identification (Machover, 1949)
2. If same sex drawing, possible striving to achieve self-control and maturity (Urban, 1963)

PERSON, APPEARING YOUNGER THAN SUBJECT

1. Possible regression; strong psychological fixations (Meyer et al., 1955)
2. Possible hysteria (McElhaney, 1969)
3. By adult male, drawing of child may indicate reserved personality (Marzolf & Kirchner, 1972)
4. If baby drawn, very severe immaturity (McElhaney, 1969)

PERSON, DEHUMANIZED (MONSTERS, ROBOTS, ETC.)

1. Possible organicity (Bruell & Albee, 1962)
2. Possible psychotic condition (Chase, 1941)
3. By children, possible psychological disturbance, perhaps acting-out, immaturity, or feelings of depersonalization (Koppitz, 1968)

PERSON, DRESSED IN CLOTHING TOO LARGE FOR FIGURE

Low self-concept (Buck, 1950)

PERSON, FACING FORWARD

Possible indication of accessibility or frankness (Machover, 1949)

PERSON, INTEGRATED POORLY

Possibility of organicity (Kahn & Giffen, 1960)

PERSON, OPPOSITE SEX, APPEARING OLDER THAN SUBJECT

Indication of sexual immaturity (Hammer, 1954)

PERSON, OVER-DRESSED

1. Narcissistic, immature tendencies, with psychosexual difficulties (Levy, 1950)
2. Social egocentricity (Machover, 1949)
3. Usually modest individual, perhaps due to repression of sex drives (Gurvitz, 1951)
4. Possible exhibitionistic tendencies (Urban, 1963)

PERSON, SEDUCTIVE

1. By preadolescents, possible normality (Machover, 1960)
2. Sometimes associated with narcissistic, and perhaps hysterical females (McElhaney, 1969)

PERSON, UNDER-DRESSED OR NUDE

Narcissistic, immature tendencies, with psychosexual difficulties (Levy, 1950)

PIPE

Sex symbol; if emphasized, possible preoccupation with sex (Buck, 1950)

POCKET(S), EMPHASIZED

1. In males, dependency and infantilism (Levy, 1958)
2. Affectional needs unsatisfied (Machover, 1958)
3. In females, emphasis upon independence (Urban, 1963)

POSTURE, GROTESQUE

Serious psychological instability (Allen, 1958)

POSTURE, LEANING

Somewhat insecure individual (Allen, 1958)

POSTURE, RELAXED AND STANDING

Normality (Urban, 1963)

POSTURE, RIGID

Possible anxiety; may result from attempts at careful impulse and fantasy control (Gilbert, 1969)

POSTURE, SEATED

Possible significant insecurity (Allen, 1958)

PROFILE OF MALE, WITH FEMALE DEPICTED FACING FORWARD

1. By males, readiness to expose female body while protecting self (Urban, 1963)
2. By males, if male drawing detailed, possible conflicts concerning sexuality, suggestive of immaturity in sexual matters (Machover, 1949)

PUPIL, OMITTED FROM ONE EYE ONLY

Possible psychotic condition (McElhaney, 1969)

RECREATIONAL EQUIPMENT, EMPHASIS ON

Possible cyclothymic tendencies (Gilbert, 1969)

RIBS, DRAWN

Possible normality (Urban, 1963)

SAME SEX DRAWING, SHADED

Possible sign of anxiety (Goldstein & Faterson, 1969)

SEX DIFFERENCES, MINIMAL

1. Possible regression (Modell, 1951)
2. By children or retardates, possible normality (Harris, 1963)

SEXUAL CHARACTERISTICS, CONFUSED

Indication of sexually maladjusted individual (King, 1954)

SHOES, EMPHASIZED

1. In males involutional syndrome, perhaps with impotency overtones (Machover, 1949)
2. If with numerous details, suggestion of an obsessive and feminine individual (Levine & Sapolsky, 1969)

SHOULDERS, BROAD IN FEMALE FIGURE AND BOSOM-LIKE IN MALE FIGURE

By males, confusion regarding sex roles (Machover, 1949)

SHOULDERS, EMPHASIZED

By females, possible masculine protest (Urban, 1963)

SHOULDERS, POINTED

Tendency to act-out (Hammer, 1969)

SHOULDERS, REINFORCED OR HESITANTLY DRAWN

Overconcern with masculinity (Levine & Sapolsky, 1969)

SHOULDERS, VERY BROAD

Tendency to act-out; possibility of aggression or uncertainty about sexual feelings; may be an attempt at compensation (Levy, 1950)

SNOWMAN AND PEANUT-MAN

When subject apparently approaches testing situation seriously, possible evasive behavior, likely to be related to problems regarding body image (Rosenzweig & Kogan, 1949)

STICK FIGURE

1. Possible insecurity, likely to be expressed by evasive behavior (Buck, 1948)
2. Uncooperative attitude (King, 1954)
3. Difficulties in relating to other people, possibly with psychopathic tendencies (Deabler, 1969)

TIE, EMPHASIZED

1. Concern with sexuality, perhaps because of feelings of inadequacy, (Hammer, 1954)
2. Unusual concern with sexuality, perhaps because of homosexual conflict (Buck, 1950)

TOES, ENCIRCLED BY LINE

Aggression may be repressed (Urban, 1963)

TOES, ON CLOTHED FIGURE
Probable aggression (Goldstein & Rawn, 1957)

TOES, POINTED
Possible feelings of aggression (Hammer, 1954)

TROUSER FLY, EMPHASIZED
Concern or conflict regarding sexuality (McElhaney, 1969)

TROUSERS, TRANSPARENT
Possibility of panic concerning homosexuality (Machover, 1949)

TRUNK, INCOMPLETELY CLOSED AT BOTTOM
1. Preoccupation with sex (Urban, 1963)
2. Possible conflict in sexuality (Jolles, 1964)

TRUNK OF FEMALE FIGURE, SHADED
By males, denial of bodily drives, with aggressive feelings toward females; most notable if female drawn first (Machover, 1949)

TRUNK, ROUND
Somewhat feminine orientation (Gurvitz, 1951)

TRUNK, SHADED, IN FEMALE FIGURE
Most notably if in first drawing by male, rejection of body drives, with aggression toward females (Machover, 1949)

TRUNK, SQUARE
Possible schizoid conditions (Reis et al., 1966)

TRUNK, UNUSUALLY THIN
If in drawing of own sex, feeling that own physique is inadequate; probable feelings of inferiority (Jolles, 1952)

WAISTLINE, SHADED HEAVILY
Conflict over sexual activities (Buck, 1966)

WEAPONS
Possible hostility and acting-out behavior, perhaps with psychopathic tendencies (Gilbert, 1969)

# BIBLIOGRAPHY

Allen, R. M. *Personality assessment procedures.* New York: Harper, 1958.

Alschuler, A. & Hattwick, W. *Painting and personality.* Chicago: University of Chicago Press, 1947.

Armon, V. Some personality variables in overt female homosexuality. *Journal of Projective Techniques,* 1960, *24,* 292-309.

Baldwin, I. T. The head-body ratio in human figure drawings of schizophrenic and normal adults. *Journal of Projective Techniques and Personality Assessment,* 1964, *28,* 393-396.

Barnouw, V. Cross-cultural research with the House-Tree-Person test. In J. N. Buck & E. F. Hammer (Eds.), *Advances in the House-Tree-Person technique: Variations and applications.* Los Angeles: Western Psychological Services, 1969.

Bodwin, R. F. & Bruck, M. The adaptation and validation of the Draw-A-Person test as a measure of self concept. *Journal of Clinical Psychology,* 1960, *16,* 427-429.

Bradfield, R. H. The predictive validity of children's drawings. *California Journal of Educational Research,* 1964, *15,* 166-174.

Britain, S. D. Effect of manipulation of children's affect on their family drawings. *Journal of Projective Techniques and Personality Assessment,* 1970, *34,* 234-237.

Brown, F. An exploratory study of dynamic factors in the content of the Rorschach protocol. *Journal of Projective Techniques,* 1953, *17,* 251-270.

Brown, F. Adult case study: Clinical validation of the House-Tree-Person drawings of an adult case (Chronic ulcerative colitis with ileostomy). In E. F. Hammer (Ed.), *The clinical application of projective drawings.* Springfield, Illinois: Thomas, 1958, p. 261-275.

Bruell, J. H. & Albee, G. W. Higher intellectual functions in a patient with hemispherectomy for tumors. *Journal of Consulting Psychology,* 1962, *25,* 90-98.

Buck, J. N. The H-T-P technique, a qualitative and quantitative scoring manual. *Journal of Clinical Psychology,* 1948, *4,* 317-396.

Buck, J. N. *Administration and interpretation of the H-T-P test; proceedings of the H-T-P workshop held at Veterans Administration Hospital, Richmond 19, Virginia, March 31, April 1, 2, 1950.* Los Angeles: Western Psychological Services, 1950.

Buck, J. N. *The House-Tree-Person technique: Revised manual.* Los Angeles: Western Psychological Services, 1966.

Buck, J. N. The use of the H-T-P in the investigation of intra-familial conflict. In J. N. Buck & E. F. Hammer, *Advances in the House-Tree-Person technique: Variations and applications.* Los Angeles: Western Psychological Services, 1969.

Burgemeister, B. B. *Psychological techniques in neurological diagnosis.* New York: Hoeber-Harper, 1962.

Burton, A. & Sjoberg, B. The diagnostic validity of human figure drawings in schozophrenia. *Journal of Psychology,* 1964, *57,* 3-18.

Chase, J. M. A study of the drawings of a male figure made by schizophrenic patients and normal subjects. *Character and Personality,* 1941, *9,* 208-217.

Cook, M. A preliminary study of the relationship of differential treatment of male and female headsize in figure drawing to the degree of attribution of the social function of the female. *Psychology Newsletter,* 1951, *34,* 1-5.

Deabler, H. L. The H-T-P in group testing and as a screening device. In J. N. Buck, and E. F. Hammer (Eds.), *Advances in the House-Tree-Person technique: Variations and applications.* Los Angeles: Western Psychological Services, 1969.

DiLeo, J. H. *Young children and their drawings.* New York:: Brunner/Mazel, 1970.

DiLeo, J. H. *Children's drawings as diagnostic aids.* New York Brunner/Mazel, 1973.

Evans, R. B. & Marmorston, J. Psychological test signs of brain damage in cerebral thrombosis. *Psychological Reports,* 1963, *12,* 915-930.

Exner, J. E. A comparison of the human figure drawings of psychoneurotics, character disturbances, normals, and subjects experiencing experimentally-induced fear. *Journal of*

*Projective Techniques,* 1962, *26,* 392-397.

Fukada, N. Japanese children's tree drawings. In J. N. Buck & E. F. Hammer (Eds.), *Advances in the House-Tree-Person technique: Variations and applications.* Los Angeles: Western Psychological Services, 1969.

Gilbert, J. *Clinical psychological tests in psychiatric and medical practice.* Springfield, Ill.: Thomas, 1969.

Goldstein, A. P. & Rawn, M. L. The validity of interpretive signs of aggression in the drawing of the human figure. *Journal of Clinical Psychology,* 1957, *13,* 169-171.

Goldstein, H. S. & Faterson, H. F. Shading as an index of anxiety in figure drawings. *Journal of Projective Techniques and Personality Assessment,* 1969, *33,* 454-456.

Gurvitz, M. *The dynamics of psychological testing.* New York: Grune & Stratton, 1951.

Halpern, F. Diagnostic methods in childhood disorders. In B. B. Wolman (Ed.), *Handbook of clinical psychology.* New York: McGraw Hill, 1965, p. 381-408.

Hammer, E. F. An investigation of sexual symbolism: A study of H-T-P's of eugenically sterilized subjects. *Journal of Projective Techniques,* 1953, *17,* 401-413.

Hammer, E. F. An experimental study of symbolism on the Bender Gestalt. *Journal of Projective Techniques,* 1954, *18,* 335-345.

Hammer, E. F. *The clinical application of projective drawings.* Springfield, Ill.: Thomas, 1958.

Hammer, E. F. Acting out and its prediction by projective drawing assessment. In L. Abt & S. Weissman (Eds.), *Acting out.* New York: Grune & Stratton, 1965, p. 228-319.

Hammer, E. F. The use of the H-T-P in a criminal court: Predicting acting out. In J. N. Buck & E. F. Hammer (Eds.), *Advances in the House-Tree-Person technique: Variations and applications.* Los Angeles: Western Psychological Services, 1969.

Handler, L. & Reyher, J. The effects of stress on the Draw-a-Person Test. *Journal of Consulting Psychology,* 1964, *28,* 259-264.

Handler, L. & Reyher, J. Figure drawing anxiety indices: A review of the literature. *Journal of Projective Techniques,* 1965, *29,* 305-313.

Harris, D. B. *Children's drawings as measures of intellectual maturity.* New York: Harcourt, Brace & World, 1963.

Haworth, M. Responses of children to a group projective film and to the Rorschach, CAT. Despert Fables and DAP. *Journal of Projective Techniques,* 1962, *25,* 47-60.

Haworth, M. & Rabin, A. I. Miscellaneous techniques. In A. I. Rabin & M. Haworth (Eds.), *Projective techniques with children.* New York: Grune & Stratton, 1960.

Heberlein M. & Marcuse, F. L. Personality variables in the DAP. *Journal of Consulting Psychology,* 1963, *27,* 461.

Hetherington, R. The effects of E.C.T. on the drawings of depressed patients. *Journal of Mental Science,* 1952, *98,* 450-453.

Hiler, E. W. & Nesvig, D. An evaluation of criteria used by clinicians to infer pathology from figure drawings. *Journal of Consulting Psychology,* 1965, *29,* 520-529.

Holzberg, J. D. & Wexler, M. The validity of human form drawings as a measure of personality deviation. *Journal of Projective Techniques,* 1950, *14,* 343-361.

Jacks, I. The clinical application of the H-T-P in criminological settings. In J. N. Buck & E. F. Hammer (Eds.), *Advances in the House-Tree-Person technique: Variations and applications.* Los Angeles: Western Psychological Services, 1969.

Johnson, J. H. Bender-Gestalt constriction as an indicator of depression in psychotic patients. *Journal of Personality Assessment,* 1973, *37,* 53-55.

Jolles, I. *A catalogue for the qualitative interpretation of the H-T-P.* Los Angeles: Western Psychological Services, 1952.

Jolles, I. *A catalogue for the qualitative interpretation of the H-T-P* (Revised). Los Angeles: Western Psychological Services, 1964.

Jolles, I. *A catalogue for the qualitative interpretation of the H-T-P.* (Revised). Los Angeles: Western Psychological Services, 1971.

Jordan, S. Projective Drawings in a cerebellar disorder due to chicken pox encephalitis. *Journal of Projective Techniques and Personality Assessment,* 1970, *34,* 256-258.

Judson, A. J. & MacCasland, B. A note on the influence of the season on tree drawings. *Journal of Clinical Psychology,* 1960, *16,* 171-173.

Kadis, A. Finger painting as a projective technique. In L. E. Abt & L. Bellak (Eds.), *Projective psychology.* New York: Knopf, 1950, p. 403-431.

Kahn, T. C. & Giffen, M. B. *Psychological techniques in diagnosis and evaluation.* New York: Pergamon, 1960.

King, F. W. The use of drawings of the human figure as an adjunct in psychotherapy. *Journal of Clinical Psychology,* 1954, *10,* 65-69.

Koch, C. *The tree test.* New York: Grune & Stratton, 1952.

Kokonis, N. D. Body image disturbance in schizophrenia: A Study of arms and feet. *Journal of Personality Assessment,* 1972, *36,* 573-575.

Koppitz, E. M. Emotional indicators on human figure drawings of children: A validation study. *Journal of Clinical Psychology,* 1966, *22,* 313-315.

Koppitz, E. M. *Psychological evaluation of children's human figure drawings.* New York: Grune & Stratton, 1968.

Lakin, M. Certain formal characteristics of human figure drawings by institutionalized aged and by normal children. *Journal of Consulting Psychology,* 1956, *20,* 471-474.

Landisberg, S. The use of the H-T-P in a mental hygiene clinic for children. In J. N. Buck & E. F. Hammer (Eds.), *Advances in the House-Tree-Person technique: Variations and applications.* Los Angeles: Western Psychological Services, 1969.

Levine, A. & Sapolsky, A. the use of the H-T-P as an aid in the screening of hospitalized patients. In J. N. Buck & E. F. Hammer (Eds.), *Advances in the House-Tree-Person technique: Variations and applications.* Los Angeles: Western Psychological Services, 1969.

Levine, M. & Galanter, E. H. A note on the "tree and trauma" interpretation in the H-T-P. *Journal of Consulting Psychology,* 1953, *17,* 74-75.

Levy, S. Figure drawing as a projective test. In L. E. Abt & L. Bellak (Eds.), *Projective psychology.* New York: Knopf, 1950, p. 257-297.

Levy, S. Projective figure drawing. In E. Hammer (Ed.), *The clinical application of projective drawings.* Springfield, Ill.: Thomas, 1958, p. 83-112; p. 135-161.

Machover, K. *Personality projection in the drawings of the human figure*. Springfield, Ill.: Thomas, 1949.

Machover, K. Drawings of the human figure: A method of personality investigation. In H. H. Anderson and Gladys Anderson (Eds.), *An introduction to projective techniques*. Englewood Cliffs, N. J.: Prentice-Hall, 1951, p. 341-369.

Machover, K. The body image in art communication as seen William Steig's drawings. *Journal of Projective Techniques*, 1955, *19*, 453-460.

Machover, K. Adolescent case study: a disturbed adolescent girl. In, E. F. Hammer (Ed.) *The clinical application of projective drawings*. Springfield, Ill.: Thomas, 1958, p. 130-134.

Machover, K. Sex differences in the developmental pattern of children seen in Human Figure Drawings. In A. I. Rabin & M. Haworth (Eds.), *Projective techniques with children*. New York: Grune & Stratton, 1960.

Marzolf, S. S. & Kirchner, J. H. House-Tree-Person drawings and personality traits. *Journal of Personality Assessment*, 1972, *36*, 148-165.

McElhaney, M. *Clinical psychological assessment of the human figure drawing*. Springfield, Ill.: Thomas, 1969.

McHugh, A. Children's figure drawings in neurotic and conduct disturbances. *Journal of Clinical Psychology*, 1966, *22*, 219-221.

Melikian, L. H. & Wahab, A. Z. First-drawn picture: A cross-culture investigation of the DAP. *Journal of Projective Techniques and Personality Assessment*, 1969, *33*, 539-541.

Meyer, B. C., Brown, F. & Levine, A. Observations on the House-Tree-Person drawing test before and after surgery. *Psychosomatic Medicine*, 1955, *17*, 428-454.

Michal-Smith, H. & Morgenstern, M. The use of the H-T-P with the mentally retarded child in a hospital clinic. In J. N. Buck & E. F. Hammer (Eds.), *Advances in the House-Tree-Person technique: Variations and applications*. Los Angeles: Western Psychological Services, 1969.

Modell, A. H. Changes in human figure drawings by patients with arterial hypertension, peptic ulcer, and bronchial asthma. *Psychosomatic Medicine*, 1949, *11*, 282-292.

Modell, A. H. Changes in human figure drawings by patients who recover from regressed states. *American Journal of Orthopsychiatry*, 1951, *21*, 584-596.

Mogar, R. E. Anxiety indices in human figure drawings. *Journal of Consulting Psychology*, 1962, *26*, 108.

Mundy, J. The use of projective techniques with children. In B. B. Wolman (Ed.), *Manual of child psychopathology*. New York: McGraw-Hill, 1972, p. 791-819.

Mursell, G. R. The use of the H-T-P with the mentally deficient. In J. N. Buck & E. F. Hammer (Eds.), *Advances in the House-Tree-Person technique: Variations and applications*. Los Angeles: Western Psychological Services, 1969.

Ogdon, D. P. *Psychodiagnostics and personality assessment: A handbook*. Los Angeles: Western Psychological Services, 1967.

Ogdon, D. P. *Psychodiagnostics and personality assessment: A handbook/second edition*. Los Angeles: Western Psychological Services, 1975.

Payne, J. J. Comments on the analysis of chromatic drawings, *Journal of clinical psychology*, Monograph Supplements, 1948, *5*, 119-120.

Pollitt, E., Hirsch, S. & Money, J. Priapism, impotence and human figure drawing. *Journal of Nervous and Mental Disease*, 1964, *139*, 161-168.

Precker, J. A. Painting and drawing in personality assessment. *Journal of Projective Techniques*, 1950, *14*, 262-286.

Reznikoff, M. & Nicholas, A. An evaluation of human-figure drawing indicators of paranoid pathology. *Journal of Consulting Psychology*, 1958, *20*, 395-397.

Reznikoff, M. & Tomblen, D. The use of human figure drawings in the diagnosis of organic pathology. *Journal of Consulting Psychology*, 1956, *20*, 467-470.

Ries, H. A., Johnson, M. H., Armstrong, H. & Holmes, D. S. The Draw-A-Person test and process reactive schizophrenia. *Journal of Projective Techniques and Personality Assessment*, 1966, *30*, 184-186.

Roback, H. & Webersinn, A. Size of figure drawings of depressed psychiatric patients. *Journal of Abnormal Psychology*, 1955, *71*, 416.

Rosenzweig, S. & Kogan, K. *Psychodiagnosis*. New York: Grune & Stratton, 1949.

Schildkrout, M. S., Shenker, I. R. & Sonnenblick, M. *Human figure drawings in adolescence*. New York: Brunner/Mazel, 1972.

Shneidman, E. S. Some relationships between thematic and drawing materials. In E. F. Hammer (Ed.), *The clinical application of projective drawings*. Springfield, Ill.: Thomas, 1958, p. 620-627.

Small, L. *Neuropsychodiagnosis in psychotherapy*. New York: Brunner/Mazel, 1973.

Urban, W. H. *The Draw-A-Person catalogue for interpretive analysis*. Los Angeles: Western Psychological Services, 1963.

Waehner, T. S. Interpretation of spontaneous drawings and paintings. *Genetic Psychology Monographs*, 1946, *33*, 3-70.

Weider, A. & Noller, P. Objective studies of children's drawings of human figures. II. Sex, age, intelligence. *Journal of Clinical Psychology*, 1953, *9*, 20-23.

Wildman, R. W. The relationship between knee and arm joints on human figure drawings and paranoid trends. *Journal of Clinical Psychology*, 1963, *19*, 460-461.

Wolff, W. *Personality of the pre-school child*. New York: Grune & Stratton, 1946.

Wolk, R. L. Projective drawings (H-T-P) of aged people. In J. N. Buck & E. F. Hammer (Eds.), *Advances in the House-Tree-Person technique: Variations and applications*. Los Angeles: Western Psychological Services, 1969.

Wolman, B. B. *Children without childhood: A study in childhood schizophrenia*. New York: Grune & Stratton, 1970.

Wysocki, B. A. & Whitney, E. Body image of crippled children as seen in Draw-a-Person test behavior. *Perceptual and Motor Skills*, 1965, *21*, 499-504.

Zimmerman, J. & Garfinkle, L. Preliminary study of the art productions of adult psychotics. *Psychiatric Quarterly*, 1942, *16*, 313-318.